פרידת רות

Pereidas Rus

Lessons in Emunah from the Weekly Parashah

in Memory of Ruti Sova, a"h

לעילוי נשמת

רות מוריה בת אריה לוי יוסף ע"ה

ISBN 10: 1-892615-24-X
ISBN 13: 978-1-892615-24-4

A Hebrew Theological College publication
7135 Carpenter Rd
Skokie, IL 60077
847-982-2500
http://www.htc.edu

Publishing services provided by JewishSelfPublishing.
www.jewishselfpublishing.com
info@jewishselfpublishing.com

All references to Rabbi Samson Raphael Hirsch's commentary on *Chumash* refer to *The Hirsch Chumash* (New York: Feldheim, 2009), unless stated otherwise.

הַנֶּאֱהָבִים וְהַנְּעִימִם בְּחַיֵּיהֶם
וּבְמוֹתָם לֹא נִפְרָדוּ.
(שמואל־ב א, כג)

Beloved and pleasant in their lives
and not separated by death.
(*Shmuel* II 1:23)

CONTENTS

FOREWORD

RABBI ZEV COHEN

MARA D'ASRA, CONGREGATION ADAS YESHURUN

CHICAGO, ILLINOIS

Adapted from his sichah delivered at the levayah le'ilui nishmas Ruti, a"h

THERE ARE A LOT OF *shailos* about saying *hespedim* for a child who passes away young. According to Rabbi Moshe Feinstein, *zt"l*, a father may give a *hesped*, but others may not.

There is a story about Rabbi Yaakov Kamenetsky, *zt"l*, who was attending the *levayah* of a young mother. He explained that that *levayah* was a *nisayon* in *emunah*. Klal Yisrael has been walking along the road of tests since its beginnings. At the *Akeidah*, Avraham Avinu said, "*Neilchah ad koh*—We will go until here" (*Bereishis* 22:5). Rashi is bothered by the word *koh*. He says it means *derech mu'at*, not too far. Then he quotes a midrash that says Avraham walked to the *Akeidah* with the word *koh* because he had a question regarding it. Hashem had said, "*Koh yihyeh zarecha*—So will be your children" (ibid. 15:5), and Avraham had asked, "How can I have children if You are telling me I need to take my only child to the *Akeidah*?" Avraham would walk to the *Akeidah* until he would get the answer to the word *koh*: "*Neilchah ad koh*." What an incredible walk.

Another person in the Torah took a walk; this was Lot. Lot said, "I'm going to walk away from Avraham and his God." He intended to walk to a place that Rashi describes using the term *shetufei zimah*, a place full of lust and desire. Here we have two people who were related to each other but took two entirely different types of walks. One walked "*neilchah ad koh*" and another walked away from *koh*.

There is a little town in Illinois named Rock Island; my mother-in-law is from there. In that town is a cemetery. In the front of the cemetery you can see a little area where children are buried. I always think, *What gave the people of Rock Island the strength to put their nisyonos in the forefront?*

My great-grandfather died when I was nineteen and he was ninety-nine. When he came to America in 1904, he had never learned in yeshivah; he had served in the czar's army and ran away. One of the first things he did when he came to America was build a shul on the farm he owned. He built the shul despite never having had the opportunity to learn in a yeshivah. He constructed it so that it had twelve windows: five windows in the north, five in the south, and two in the east. This is the way halachah instructs us to build them, but most aren't able to due to various limitations. Whenever I saw that shul I was always amazed by that.

People can walk through life with *nisyonos* and take the strength that we have in our DNA from Avraham Avinu. Not everyone makes the walk or completes the walk, but many have and many continue to do so.

There was another person in *Tanach* who walked as well. Her name was Rus. Rus had a choice. She could have walked away from her mother-in-law, Naomi, but she made a different choice, uttering the words, "*El asher teilchi eileich*—Toward wherever you will walk, I will walk" (*Rus* 1:16). What an incredible walk.

Our Rus, Ruti, also walked. The name Chaya was added shortly after she was in the hospital; she became Rus Chaya Moriah. Taking the first letter of the three words in her name in a slightly different order, we have רמח, *ramach*, which has the same *gematria* as the words "Avraham Avinu." Ruti took exactly the same walk that Avraham Avinu did.

At the *Akeidah*, Avraham said, "*Shevu lachem poh im hachamor*—Stay here with the donkey" (*Bereishis* 22:5). The word *chamor* has the same letters: חמר. A person has a choice. He can ask: "How am I going to walk: *ramach*, like Avraham or *chamor*, like Lot? Will I choose the walk that can take me to *ruchniyus* like Avraham, or to *gashmiyus* like Lot?" Avraham walked with Yitzchak *ad koh*.

I asked my rabbe'im: When adding to Ruti's name, where should we put the name Chaya—at the beginning, at the end, or in the middle? I spoke to a rebbe who thought to put it in the middle, Rus Chaya Moriah, so that the first letters of each name spell *rachem*.

Ruti's parents, Aryeh and Shoshana, displayed incredible grace in walking on this very difficult road every day. Every day, every step, every inch was an unbelievable walk. They showed tremendous strength, individually and together. They walked the walk of *ramach*, the walk of Avraham, and the walk of Rus. There were enormous questions, which they brought to *talmidei chachamim*. There were extraordinary challenges, which they brought to doctors who were also *talmidei chachamim*. Throughout all of these *nisyonos*, Aryeh and Shoshana continued on the walk.

The word *levayah* means to accompany someone, to walk with them. I find this concept interesting regarding Ruti. We walk behind and the *meis* leads. This is because in a very special way, Ruti, Rus Chaya Moriah, taught us how to walk in the way of Avraham and in the way of Rus.

No one should have to take this walk, but in life we don't get to choose the path we travel. We only choose *how* to walk that path.

The Sovas, together their children, together with their entire family, and we as a *kehillah* should be *zocheh* to walk *ad koh*, to be able to walk with *emunah* when these paths are shown to us. We should be *zocheh* that this is the last walk of this kind anyone in Klal Yisrael ever has to take. The next walk should be, as Aryeh said, to Yerushalayim Ir Hakodesh, led by Mashiach, preceded by *techiyas hameisim*. Then, all the answers to all of our questions, and all of the meanings to all of the walks, will become clear.

PREFACE

HOW DOES SOMEONE START LIVING a new life again after losing a child? The Maharal (*Nesiv Hayissurin* 2:3) accurately describes how losing one's child is as if part of the parents' own bodies is forever lost, as a child is literally an extension of the parents themselves.[1] Losing a beautiful, innocent, and perfect child is incomprehensible enough, but the death of a young child is considered a greater tragedy since this loss is not just the end of one life; it's as if multitudes have died due to all potential future generations that are also now gone (*Ben Yehoyada, Zevachim* 115b). How do we continue on with this gaping hole at our Shabbos table, in our home, in our hearts? With all this pain, loss, hurt, and confusion, how can one move forward?[2]

I don't know.

Yet in that dark space of doubt and uncertainty is where faith needs to kick in. Faith can start only at the point where empirical knowledge ends. In *Emunah U'bitachon* (2:2) the Chazon Ish, *zt"l*, writes about

---

1. In contrast to a spouse, who is only considered *kegufo*, like part of one's body, a child is actually part of a parent's body.

2. Rabbi Moshe Feinstein discusses how a crisis of faith in the wake of a child's death can be so devastating that it can even be considered a life-threatening situation. In *Iggeros Moshe* (*Yoreh Dei'ah*, vol. 2, 174:1), he quotes the Ri found in *Tosafos* (*Bava Metzia* 114b), who says that the only way Eliyahu Hanavi was allowed to be *metamei* himself to revive the lifeless child of a widow was because it involved *pikuach nefesh*, which supersedes the prohibition against becoming *tamei*. Rabbi Moshe explains that when the Ri invoked the concern of *pikuach nefesh*, he was not referring to saving the child's life, since he was no longer living; rather, the concern was about his mother's survival. Eliyahu revived the child and allowed himself to become *tamei* in the process because he was concerned about the vulnerability of this widow, who would be shattered after she dedicated herself so much to Hashem's *navi* and to her faith in Hashem and yet lost her child. Eliyahu thus revived the child to save the widow's life.

how it is easy for someone to spout words of faith and trust when it's just theoretical and impractical; over time, a person can become convinced that he has achieved lofty levels of faith, superior even to his peers. However, he writes, the true test of a person's relationship with Hashem occurs when a very difficult challenge arises and one is forced to face whether his faith is based on fanciful dreams or whether it is sincere and he truly relies on Hashem.

After our tragedy, the hard work of rebuilding faith began. During shivah for Ruti, *a"h*, a prominent *rav* from Eretz Yisrael told me and Shoshana that, after the loss of one of his children, he told all of his *chavrusos* that they must change whatever they had been learning and instead only delve into topics of *emunah* moving forward. This was comforting and very relatable for us. Losing our beautiful Ruti in such a traumatic manner changed us and our lives forever. Our lives seemed to be following one path, when suddenly, shockingly, our personal *ananei hakavod* veered sharply in a radical new direction, sending us onto a drastically different journey. Now the ground beneath our feet feels less firm, the world seems to spin on an altered axis, time moves slower and quicker at the same time, and nothing seems normal anymore. Every day the battle to survive begins again, fighting the darkness, stumbling through the confusion, and again desperately trying to locate and hold tight to the faith that binds us with our Creator. We are left with hundreds of unanswerable questions. Why? Why us? Why her?

I don't know. For the rest of my life, I will never know.

Maybe this state of not knowing, of saying nothing, of leaving the answer blank, is itself an expression of deep *emunah*. In the wake of the unthinkable double personal tragedy Aharon Hakohen experienced, which took place on a national stage, he is recognized and rewarded for his silence: "*Vayidom Aharon*" (*Vayikra* 10:3). Why was silence the response which earned praise and privilege, rather than a bold declaration of *tzidduk hadin*, of the righteousness of Hashem's judgment?[3]

---

3. See *Torah Temimah, Koheles* 3:7, who raises a similar question.

Isn't silence simply a lack of response?

When Hashem wanted to reveal His glory to Eliyahu Hanavi, we see parallels to what occurred when Aharon's sons were killed, and both narratives are linked by using the same root word, *dom* (see *Melachim I* 19:12). As Eliyahu perched himself at the edge of a cave, Hashem demonstrated brutal destruction—rock-shattering winds, a rumbling earthquake, a blazing fire—and within it, He could not be found. Finally, after the cacophony of destruction, Eliyahu could discern a *"kol demamah dakah*—a still, small sound" (ibid.) and that is where Hashem's glory was finally found. As Rashi emphasizes (*"kol haba mitoch hademamah"*), Eliyahu did not simply hear nothing; rather, he heard the sound of silence.[4] Again, we find shocking destruction followed by a silence that reveals Hashem's greatness. This silence is not simply the absence of sound, but is a powerful response that needs to be listened to carefully.

Why is the sound of silence in the aftermath of calamity the best path to finding Hashem again? Perhaps one more example of the word *dom* can help illuminate the depth and nature of this particular form of silence. In chapter 37 of *Tehillim*, David Hamelech teaches us how to live in trying circumstances. He first tells us, *"U'vetach alav vehu ya'aseh*—Trust in Him and He will do it" (*Tehillim* 37:5). Then he implores, *"Dom laHashem vehis'cholel lo*—Be silent [for Hashem's salvation] and place your hope in Him" (ibid. 37:7).[5] The commentators on this verse define *dom* as a special type of silence; it is quiet meditation suffused with hope, anticipating Hashem's answer and the moment He will shine His light on us.

Dom means to silently maintain faith in Hashem's ways and in one's own future even in the face of tremendous suffering. It is a hope that cannot possibly be articulated with words and logic at the moment of

---

4. Rambam in his commentary on *Avos* 3:3 connects Aharon's response with Hashem's revelation to Eliyahu.

5. The Gemara in *Zevachim* (115b) links Aharon's *dom* response to this *pasuk* in *Tehillim*.

suffering, but it is hope that still stirs somewhere within us.[6] Words encapsulate, limit, define; hope in the face of tragedy defies easy definitional properties. If the hope were expressed in words, this deep inner faith, an almost illogical hope, would become constricted, distorted, subject to analysis and empiricism. The silence of *dom* is not the absence of response; it is an empathic but silent statement of inexpressible strength.

Ruti's great-great-great-great-grandfather, Rabbi Samson Raphael Hirsch, *zt"l*, poignantly describes (on *Bamidbar* 9:16) how the Jewish nation's long travels through the arid desert helped cultivate this national trait of "quiet, serene resignation and trusting patience" in order to help the Jewish people withstand the harsh suffering of the future exiles. The Torah stresses that the nation's patience while waiting to proceed in their travels through the wilderness until the *ananei hakavod* led the way was actually the ultimate evidence of their obedience to Hashem, even more than the faithful following of the clouds to wherever they led. The message is clear, and Rabbi Hirsch's words ring with a truthful clarity that resonate even more deeply after saying goodbye to our dear daughter:

> At times He instructs us to leave what we have just now begun to love, and at times He requires us to remain steadfast in an undesirable situation… We will always be ready to put all our trust in Hashem and to follow Him to unknown destinations, along mysterious paths; to wait and long for Him patiently, or to follow Him boldly—all according to the direction of His guidance.[7]

---

6. See also *Nachalas Avos* 3:3.

7. Of course, this ideal of faithful, patient, hopeful waiting is a common theme frequently stressed in Judaism; for example: "*Ani maamin bevias haMashiach ve'af al pi sheyismameihah im kol zeh achakeh lo bechol yom sheyavo*—I believe in the coming of Mashiach and even though he may be delayed, despite this, I eagerly await his arrival every day" (*Rambam peirush mishnayos* to *Perek Chelek*) or "*Lishuasecha kivisi Hashem*—For Your salvation I hope for, Hashem" (*Bereishis* 49:18).

The Torah describes the Jewish people's first battle against Amalek, evil personified. In the *pasuk* when Moshe was growing weary; when his arms were becoming heavy; when gravity, fatigue, time, and pain were all pushing against him, dragging his hands down—the term *emunah* is used. As long as the battle against Amalek continued, he strained to continue holding his arms aloft until the sun set (*Shemos* 17:12):

וִידֵי מֹשֶׁה כְּבֵדִים וַיִּקְחוּ אֶבֶן וַיָּשִׂימוּ תַחְתָּיו וַיֵּשֶׁב עָלֶיהָ וְאַהֲרֹן וְחוּר תָּמְכוּ בְיָדָיו מִזֶּה אֶחָד וּמִזֶּה אֶחָד וַיְהִי יָדָיו אֱמוּנָה עַד בֹּא הַשָּׁמֶשׁ.

> The hands of Moshe became heavy; and they took a stone and placed it under him, and he sat upon it. Aharon and Chur supported his hands, one on either side, and so his hands remained an expression of trust until the sun set.

Emunah is the strength to stand up in the darkness despite all of the pain and suffering, when everything is pushing us back down, and simply continuing on as long as the battle persists. Our job is to see through the loud, ravaging storms and find the shelter of still silence, which somehow carries hope within it. I don't know and yet I continue. This is *emunah*.[8]

Some experts in trauma recommend that one who has experienced a tragedy should try to cultivate a perspective that tragedies occur randomly, as a way to avoid personalizing the event. David Kessler, a leading grief specialist, writes about the tragic loss of his own adult son: "[T]his loss had happened to me, it was not because of me. And I was

---

8. Even those who comfort mourners are instructed to sit in silence, at least until they are acknowledged by the mourner. *Revid Hazahav* (*Vayikra* 10:3) uses Aharon's silence as a source for the Gemara in *Berachos* (6b): "*Amar Rav Papa agra devai tamya—shesikusa*," that one who visits a house of mourning should sit in silence (see *Yoreh Dei'ah* 376:1). This is the comfort provided by silent consolers: We do not know either, but we are here, by your side, holding you up, helping you continue, giving you hope.

not unique in my suffering, either; had not been singled out by God or fate or whatever to undergo this ordeal."[9]

As believing Jews committed to Torah ideals, we do not have this option to simply claim we are not being singled out when tragedy befalls us. Contrast Mr. Kessler's words with Rabbi Aharon Lichtenstein's description about how people of faith confront tragedies:

> Hazal took it as a matter of course that one should regard personal suffering in the context of one's relation to the *Ribbono shel Olam*. But as to conjecture concerning its substantive significance, they acknowledged considerable latitude... Perhaps that is precisely the point: the range of perception and interpretation. One can rule out neither the chastising rod nor the stroking palm, and hence none of the correlative emotions. Various possibilities are to be entertained and examined, with no assurance that the uncertainty will be resolved.[10]

The silence of not knowing, never understanding, and yet grappling and undertaking intense and unresolvable introspection is more challenging, and less neat, than simply ascribing tragedy to the randomness of the universe. But a believer does not have simple explanatory models.[11]

I took the mitzvah and *avodah* of *emunah* for granted before we lost our Ruti, of course—the blessing afforded someone with an openly charmed life. I believed because I did, and any questions or challenges I had about faith were purely intellectual. Going through what we have and what we continue to experience, we will never be the same, and we

---

9. David Kessler, *Finding Meaning: The Sixth Stage of Grief* (New York: Scribner, 2019), 244.

10. Rabbi Aharon Lichtenstein, "The Duties of the Heart and Response to Suffering," in *Leaves of Faith: The World of Jewish Living*, vol. 2 (New York: Ktav Publishing House, 2004), 132.

11. Obviously this is not the setting for an in-depth discussion of concepts like *hashgachah pratis, bechirah, teva,* and *mikreh.*

must never be the same people we were before. Now that my *emunah* is being challenged and weighed down by the most intense emotional pain and confusion, I'm being forced to develop new reservoirs of resilience I never had before, and I'm being shaken awake in order to re-examine the priorities and direction of my life.

I've also been forced to deepen and expand my relationship with Hashem on a daily basis. This new relationship requires much harder work. I can now begin to recognize the beauty of the intimacy of *emunah*. Like in all authentic relationships, privacy, honesty, hard work, and deep introspection are required. Some days I feel close and, on others, I feel very alone. Some days, instead of hearing the sound of silence, it feels like I hear nothing at all.

When I feel stronger, Hashem is the greatest therapist possible, and I can turn to Him in all pain and just talk, even without seeking an answer, as it says in *Tehillim* (142:3), "*Eshpoch lefanav sichi tzarasi lefanav agid*—I pour out my hardships[12] before Him; I declare my distress before Him." No one really knows my confusion, my daily struggles, my hourly pain like He does, and that has made me cherish the hard work of faith more than I ever have before. So many questions will always remain, so much confusion may always reign, but through *emunah* I can always reclaim a secret connecting bond between me and Hashem, a silent hope and faith no one else is privy to. When I cannot find the words to express my faith, I can continue to bend myself against the forces of gravity and find Hashem in the quiet stillness of hope.

In contrast to the silent response, this *sefer* is a loud, resounding reaction to a tragedy. This work is how a global community responds to the pain of one of its own, with care and support, and through the eternal guidance of the Torah. We feel so embraced by so many coming together during this time of painful separation.

Shoshana, Eyli, Noa, Rina, and I are so grateful to the organizers, editors (including Yossi Goldin, Zvi Herman, and Mike Wiesenberg),

---

12. See *Metzudas Tzion*.

contributing authors, financial supporters, and true *chaverim* for spending so much effort, time, and care in producing this *sefer*. We especially want to thank the editors Ari Bajtner and Daniel Weiss for spearheading this project with such sensitivity and dedication, generously devoting their time and energy to ensure the timely publication of this meaningful and powerful *sefer*. Thank you deeply to all of those who contributed in any way to this especially meaningful project, including my rabbe'im and friends; to Hebrew Theological College for providing a platform for this *sefer* to be published; and to the staff of JewishSelf-Publishing for all of their support.

While the *sefer* could have better reflected who Ruti was by focusing on *middos* she exemplified, such as *simchah*, we believe it is a great *zechus* for her that the *divrei Torah* to follow mostly focus on some element of *emunah*. We hope this *sefer* serves as one means of inspiring more frequent and deeper conversations of *emunah* and greater demonstrations of faith within our homes. We hope, despite the pain, sadness, and confusion, that Ruti's memory can continue inspiring others to focus on the blessings of an openly (or more hidden) charmed life; that she can continue helping individuals and families deepen their awareness of their relationship with, and their enduring faith in our Father in Heaven, leading to lives filled with an exuberant joy she loudly and proudly demonstrated during her few years with us.

Aryeh Sova

INTRODUCTION

BY ARYEH SOVA

THE TERM *PEREIDAH* IS USED in several contexts in relation to Rus. When describing why the entire nation of Moav was worthy of being spared, the Gemara (*Bava Kamma* 38a–b) explains they were all saved because of one *pereidah tovah*, a good young bird,[1] who would eventually descend from them: Rus. In the Chida's *sefer* on *Megillas Rus*, *Simchas Haregel*, he offers an additional layer of interpretation of this particular term: *Pereidah* refers to separation. Rus, he explains, had a special, distinct *neshamah* filled with *kedushah* that made her unique and separate, and Hashem eventually specifically chose and separated her from among others. The title of this *sefer* refers to our pure, precious, young Ruti, who had a special and utterly unique *neshamah* and who was specifically chosen to return to Shamayim.

The term *pereidah* is also an allusion to death. Rus referred to death as a *pereidah*, a separation. She told Naomi that she would cling tightly to her and that the only thing that would separate them is death: "*Ki hamaves yafrid beini u'veineich*" (*Rus* 1:17). Death is certainly a separation on several planes. On one level, it is the parting of the physical body and the *neshamah*. However, ultimately this separation is only temporary, as one day there will be a reunion between body and *neshamah* at *techiyas hameisim*.[2]

On another level, death is of course the separation between the living and the one who passed away. But this is also not a true, permanent detachment. As the Malbim points out, Rus was passionately stating her desire to convert, so that even in their deaths, she and Naomi would

---

1. *Rashi. Zohar Chadash*, *Rus* 6 and 141, points out that the name Rus (רות) is the reverse of the word *tor* (תור), turtledove, since she was kosher and pure like a turtledove.
2. See, for example, *Derech Hashem* 1:3:11.

never be truly separated and would thus always remain connected in the next world as well.

Despite being missed deeply in this world, we know we are simply and temporarily physically separated from Ruti, while she continues and is not truly gone. The Ohr Hachaim (*Devarim* 14:1) writes a parable to help us understand why saying we have lost someone is an incorrect way to understand the death of a loved one: A father sends his son to a distant city to buy some merchandise. After a while, seeing that his son does not return, the father then sends someone to try to find him. However, the father doesn't realize that the son's absence was felt only in his hometown; this doesn't mean that he no longer exists. The son did not return because he is better off in his new home, as he is closer to his original Father (Hashem), the Source of all life.

Of course, with every beat of our hearts, we long for the day when we will one day reunite with our Ruti. However, we also live every day knowing that while we may be physically separated, we are still deeply connected with her, even in this world.

Like in the Ohr Hachaim's parable, the Lubavitcher Rebbe, *zt"l*, told a despondent father who had lost a son that he should imagine the son was living in a foreign country and could no longer communicate with his father, but he could rest assured that all of the son's needs were being attended to and that he was enduring no suffering. Although the separation was difficult, a father would be happy for his child in these circumstances. The Rebbe then stressed that, though separated, a connection could remain, as each *tefillah* recited and every mitzvah done was a gift sent to the child that continued their true connection. In a letter, the Rebbe wrote, "The connection between the living in this world and the soul who has ascended continues to exist, for the soul is enduring and eternal, and it sees and contemplates what is occurring with those connected with her and close to her" (*Toras Menahem—Menachem Tzion*, vol. 2, p. 543). This *sefer*, *Pereidas Rus*, lovingly put together by friends and *rabbanim le'ilui nishmas* Ruti, is the most beautiful present a community can deliver and a resounding testament to our everlasting connection.

Rabbi Yerucham Levovitz, *zt"l*, wrote a letter to his nephew, who was grieving over the loss of his father. In emphatic terms, he told his nephew that a fundamental belief of Judaism is that "there are no separations between this world and the World to Come, and there are no separations between the living and the dead." He continued, describing how when someone dies, they are not truly gone: "On the contrary, they are even closer now and they are even more present with us than when they were living, since no barrier exists between them anymore. [The deceased] is living, close, and present with us always."

Rashi (*Vayikra* 23:36) famously uses a description of the pain a parent feels when separating from a child to describe the message behind Shemini Atzeres. In the metaphor, when the time came for the king's children to leave him, the king implored them to stay for one more day, since "*kasheh alai pereidaschem*—it is so difficult to be separated from you." Shemini Atzeres is the extra day when we, the children, stay close to our Father.

Wouldn't staying just one more day make the separation *more* difficult? Additionally, isn't it just delaying the inevitable? Perhaps this explanation of Rashi's comment uncovers several crucial points. Each day, every moment we have together, is precious and can never be taken for granted. So much can happen in a single day and seemingly nothing at all can happen within one day, but that time is still the most precious gift. It is worth every second of pain of the eventual separation for even one more day together. Each day a parent and child are with each other is a present to savor.

Additionally, receiving one "extra" day to spend together can provide an opportunity to gratefully reflect on the time spent together. Then, when the inevitable time of separation does occur, as painful as it is to say goodbye, the parents can still appreciate what they had even when it is gone.

Finally, perhaps this story teaches us that separating is of course very difficult and painful, and while we always want to hold on as long as possible, we know we will need to say goodbye one day. We continue to embrace even with the knowledge that one day we will have to let go. Loving and living carries the risk of losing. Continuing to continue in the face of loss is an act of courage.

We feel so grateful and blessed that Hashem allowed us to have over three years with our hilarious, super-smart, and uber-confident Ruti. She radiated joy. Ruti was ebullient and tough and soft. She certainly had a temper, but if you stared her down long enough, no matter how angry she was, she would always fold and start cracking up. She was always singing to herself. Ruti was so weird, in the best way possible, and she was constantly making us laugh.

She was such a brave, independent girl, it was so easy to forget how young she was. When we were frustrated, she would always tell us to be happy, and she was in such pain every time her baby sister Rina cried. She played football with Eyli, running from him as he "tried" to tackle her, and she would steal toys all the time from Noa's room, acting perfectly innocent each time. When we opened her shades in the morning, she excitedly pointed out the start of a fresh new day, exclaiming, "It is sunny today!" She insisted on putting her shoes on by herself no matter how long it took, every single time, and she put her shoes on the wrong feet, every single time; it absolutely had to be intentional.

If you knew Ruti, you knew her huge smile, which would completely take over her whole face, and you knew her messy, curly hair, which she never allowed anyone to fix. I can still feel her soft, chubby hands directing my face toward her to make sure I was granting her my full attention. I can still see her swinging her arms wildly and confidently and skipping happily along the sidewalk. Our precious, special *neshamah*.

The time we had with Ruti was so short, but the depth of our love for her is infinite, and each memory we have of her is an invaluable jewel. We miss her every moment—*kasheh aleinu pereidaseich*. We know that *pereidah* is a part of living, as difficult as it is. For anyone who experiences loss, especially for families who lose a child, that decision to continue living, evolving, growing, takes courage. Rashi is teaching us that Shemini Atzeres shows us how to savor and hold on tight to what we have, and the day after Shemini Atzeres reminds us about getting up, continuing, and starting again while coping with the pain of separation.

As we continue climbing the mountain again, we do so with full faith that while Ruti has separated from the physical realm, it is simply a separation, not an end, and she still lives, in a world infinitely greater than ours. Also, now our love for her and our relationship with her is no longer bound by physical constraints and she is now even more deeply connected with us spiritually. We live in different worlds, across different dimensions, but that separation only strengthens our love and the depth of our true connection, and that relationship will always endure.

· פרשת בראשית ·

PARASHAS BEREISHIS

MAN'S CREATION AND HIS
ULTIMATE SPIRITUAL DESTINY

BY RABBI MICHAEL ROSENSWEIG

In the immediate aftermath of man's creation *betzelem Elokim*, in the image of Hashem (*Bereishis* 1:26–27), the basis for an anthropocentric orientation, we await with eager anticipation the Torah's formulation of man's purpose, his telos. Instead, in an initially surprising, even anticlimactic, development, the Torah only records man's geographic placement in this world. After describing the ingredients, mechanism, and process of His creation: "*Vayitzor Hashem Elokim es ha'adam afar min ha'adamah vayipach be'apav nishmas chaim vayehi ha'adam lenefesh chayah—*And Hashem God created man as dust from the earth, and He blew within him a life-soul, and man became a living being" (ibid. 2:7), the Torah locates Adam in the newly minted Gan Eden: "*Vayita Hashem Elokim gan beEden mikedem vayasem sham es ha'adam asher yatzar—*And Hashem God planted a garden in Eden from Kedem, and He placed there man that He had created" (ibid. 2:8).

Only several *pesukim* later, after repeating the Gan Eden–venue focus, and substituting the more targeted and purposive verb *vayanicheihu*, and He placed him, for *vayasem* does the Torah finally address man's goal and destiny: "*Vayikach Hashem Elokim es ha'adam vayanicheihu veGan Eden le'avdah u'leshomrah—*And Hashem God took the man and placed him in Gan Eden, to work on it and to guard it" (ibid. 2:15). The employment of dual verbs "*le'avdah u'leshomrah—*to work on it and to guard it" is very significant indeed, as it succinctly captures and embodies the dialectical challenge of being both a responsible custodian tasked with preservation and stewardship as well as one who oversees the cultivation, development, and advancement of the world. This fascinating encapsulation of man's mission—"*le'avdah u'leshom-rah*"—further deepens the mystery of the Torah's initial obscure focus, especially the earlier absence of any program or spiritual charge. Why the double depiction of man's origins, and how can we account for the evident discrepancy in emphasis?

The Netziv (*Ha'amek Davar* 2:8, 15) perceives in these disparities a subtle yet profound shift in the Divine program for man. Initially the goal was simply for man to bask in and derive spiritual succor and sustenance from the Shechinah, much as Moshe Rabbeinu did at Sinai, and as the *neshamos* of the righteous enjoy in Olam Haba.[3] This transcendent experience of Hashem's presence evidently justified man's creation and provided sufficient purpose to his existence. The Netziv does not elaborate on the catalyst for the shift in Hashem's program for man, but his presentation suggests that the reformulation of "*le'avdah u'leshom-rah*" (and, by extension, "*vayanicheihu*"; see also Malbim) is linked with other changes from the initial creation vision and constitutes a significant shift in focus. It is conceivable that this change in orientation mirrors others, such as the shift in *Bereishis* from invoking the Divine Name of Elokim to Hashem, or the different iterations of the relationship between man and woman, phenomena that are discussed extensively in the commentaries.

Rather than viewing these as changes stemming from Divine disappointment, human failure, or other manifestations of altered reality, inviting the theological quandary implied by such unanticipated developments, I'd like to suggest a different perspective. The Torah, by initially de-emphasizing man's charge and accentuating the Shechinah as man's location and venue, underscores that the telos of man is both simple and profound, to attain that which is simultaneously indispensable and

---

3. *Berachos* 17a; Rambam, *Hilchos Teshuvah* 8:2: "*Tzaddikim yoshvim ve'aterosei-hem berosheihen venehenin miziv haShechinah*—Righteous people sit with crowns upon their heads and bask in the glory of the Shechinah."

impossible: an authentic bond with Hashem, Who is both immanent and transcendent. Only several *pesukim* later does the Torah provide a detailed methodology of how to merit and accomplish this loftiest of goals: *"le'avdah u'leshomrah."* The extensive, this-worldly halachic system uniquely directs man in his cultivation of this bond with Hashem. It is noteworthy that the ultimate reward for toiling in this world in compliance with the guidelines of *"le'avdah u'leshomrah"* is Olam Haba/Gan Eden, where the original formulation of *"vayasem sham es ha'adam,"* to derive pleasure *"miziv haShechinah,"* is fully realized.

The Mishnah asserts the primacy of this world as an opportunity for spiritual growth: *"Yafah sha'ah achas biteshuvah u'ma'asim tovim baOlam Hazeh mikol chayei haOlam Haba—*Better one hour of repentance and good deeds in this world than all the life in the World to Come" (*Avos* 4:22). The Mishnah states this even as it declares the ultimate superiority of the rewarding experience of Olam Haba: *"Veyafah sha'ah achas shel koras ruach baOlam Haba mikol chayei haOlam Hazeh—*And better one hour of bliss in the World to Come than the whole life of this world."* These truisms merely reflect the distinction between the vision of *"vayasem sham es ha'adam"* and the process and method of *"vayanicheihu le'avdah u'leshomrah."*

It is a significant challenge to cultivate personal spiritual-halachic growth by means of concrete involvement in the turbulent world while remaining ever cognizant that the goal is to forge a bond with Hashem, to bask in His timeless presence. Specific mitzvos obviously accentuate and directly contribute to the goal: standing before Hashem in *tefillah* and at the *mo'adim*; *aliyah laregel*; Shabbos, which is *"mei'ein Olam Haba—*a taste of the World to Come"; and others. At the same time, we should always acknowledge and continuously reinforce the principle that the halachos that govern and regulate the more physical, concrete, and even contentious facets of life are no less dedicated to, and facilitating of, the telos of taking pleasure *"miziv haShechinah."* In some ways, they achieve an even more aspirational goal by sanctifying the mundane and the material. The singular stature of Yom Kippur, the most consequential day on the calendar, a day of pure spirituality, of "*kulo laHashem*—entirely before Hashem" and "*lifnei Hashem tit'haru*—before Hashem you should purify yourself" further exemplifies the impact of the original creation ideal of "*vayasem sham es ha'adam*." We must be mindful of this orientation and focus despite, and because of, "*le'avdah u'leshomrah*."

It is striking that during the *teshuvah* period of Elul and Tishrei, when we are judged based on our actions and halachic commitment—"*le'avdah u'leshomrah*"—we constantly recite the *pasuk* in *Tehillim* (27:4) that magnificently encapsulates the vision of experiencing transcendence:

אַחַת שָׁאַלְתִּי מֵאֵת ה' אוֹתָהּ אֲבַקֵּשׁ שִׁבְתִּי בְּבֵית ה' כָּל יְמֵי חַיַּי לַחֲזוֹת בְּנֹעַם ה' וּלְבַקֵּר בְּהֵיכָלוֹ.

> One thing I ask of You, Hashem, that I request—to dwell in the House of Hashem all the days of my life, to gaze from the splendor of Hashem and to visit His Sanctuary.

Our single and singular aspiration is to bask in His presence.

The loss of a precious, irreplaceable family member is deeply painful; the loss of a beloved, precocious child whose opportunity of "*le'avdah u'leshomrah*" has been tragically cut short is simply unfathomable. Yet it's important to acknowledge that, however too brief, the life of a special person still imparts an indelible impression and bequeaths an unforgettable legacy rooted in their singular qualities and personality: the zest for life, the overflowing affection, the devotion and loyalty to family. Moreover, it is both meaningful and a source of consolation that notwithstanding the crucial contribution of the methodology of "*le'avdah u'leshomrah*," and especially in conjunction with it, life's mysterious purpose and goal remains paramount: "*Vayita Hashem Elokim gan beEden mikedem vayasem sham es ha'adam asher yatzar*." The capacity for and magnitude of deriving pleasure "*miziv haShechinah*," experiencing the presence of Hashem, remains the ultimate goal that transcends physical life—and that endures forever.

· פרשת נח ·

PARASHAS NOACH

THE POWER TO ALTER
THE COURSE OF HISTORY

BY URI GOTTLIEB

After the flood, one of Noach's first endeavors was to plant a vine-yard, as the *pasuk* relates, "*Vayachel Noach ish ha'adamah vay-ita karem*—And Noach, the man of the earth, was the first to plant a vineyard" (*Bereishis* 9:20). There is some dispute among the commentaries regarding the meaning of the word *vayachel*. Rashi is of the opinion that it is derived from the word *chullin*, desecration. According to Rashi, the beginning of the *pasuk* should be understood as follows: "And he [Noach] became desecrated." It would seem that since this was Noach's first agricultural feat in the new world, he should not have started with a vineyard, which one could abuse by becoming intoxicated from its wine.

Alternatively, the Sforno translates *vayachel* as "and he began," from the root word *techilah*, which means "beginning." The Sforno cites a proof for this definition from the *pasuk* in *Bamidbar* (25:1) which says, "*Vayachel ha'am lizenos el bnos Moav*—And the people began to commit immoral acts with the daughters of Moav." When the women of Moav attempted to lure Bnei Yisrael into idolatry, they began by ensnaring them through immorality. Only afterward did they introduce idols for the Jewish people to worship. The Sforno explains that in this context, the word *vayachel* alludes to the beginning of a process, one that can lead to unintended and sometimes extreme consequences.

In the *pasuk* in *Bamidbar*, the term *vayachel* alludes to the fact that Bnei Yisrael had no intention of worshipping idolatry when they became involved with the daughters of Moav. Nevertheless, that first misstep of immoral behavior quickly caused them to deteriorate further, until they found themselves worshipping idols. In the case of Noach, the *vayachel* process was even more drastic. Noach was given the noble task of replanting the world anew, but he made a small misstep in the wrong direction. As Rashi says, he should have started with a different crop. That one seemingly insignificant blunder started a whole sequence of events that led to the ugly episode of his son Cham seeing *ervas aviv*, the nakedness of his father, and ultimately ended with the *berachos* of Shem and Yafes and the curse of Canaan. These blessings and curses ultimately altered the entire course of human history, the effects of which we still feel today.

The lesson for us is powerful. Any slight action we take, if mixed with even the smallest amount of corruption, can set in motion a series of events which snowball toward a destructive end. Conversely, any positive action we do has the potential to initiate a chain of circumstances leading to good results. One should never disregard a small act of *chesed* or any mitzvah as inconsequential. Our deeds have the power to set off a domino effect of good that can lead to outcomes we never dreamed possible.

There are many privileged individuals within Klal Yisrael who have the *zechus* to impact thousands through their teachings or philanthropy. However, even the common folk among us must recognize that we too wield incredible power and influence, albeit on a less conspicuous scale. Every good deed, no matter how seemingly limited in scope, has the potential to literally change the world.

· פרשת לך לך ·

PARASHAS LECH LECHA

THE INSPIRATION OF AVRAHAM

BY RABBI URI LESSER

The parashah begins with Hashem's well-known commandment of "*Lech lecha*," telling Avraham Avinu to leave his home and journey toward Eretz Yisrael. This is the first time the Torah records a dialogue between Hashem and Avraham. The Ohr Hachaim asks the following question: Why did Hashem command Avraham to go before He completely revealed Himself to him? With all the other *nevi'im*, first Hashem revealed Himself to the *navi* and only afterward gave him a commandment or mission. Why didn't Hashem do that with Avraham?

The Ohr Hachaim offers two answers to this question. First, since Avraham had already found and recognized Hashem on his own, there was no need for Hashem to reveal Himself any further at this time. Rather, He wanted Avraham to leave as quickly as possible. Only afterward would He continue to reveal Himself and strengthen their relationship.

Second, the rest of the *nevi'im* already had a strengthened *emunah* and understanding of Hashem from their ancestors, teachers, and others from previous generations. Therefore, Hashem could trust, so to speak, that they would listen to Him and did not feel the need to test them before revealing Himself to them. By contrast, since Avraham had no previous teacher to guide him, and only discovered Hashem by himself, Hashem wanted to test him first before revealing Himself any further.

At first glance, these two answers seem to be polar opposites. The first reason portrays Avraham's finding Hashem on his own in a positive light: Since he already knew Hashem, he could receive the mission immediately. The second reason seems to imply the opposite: Since Avraham knew about Hashem "only" on his own, he needed to be tested.

Which one is it? Is it better or worse to discover Hashem on your own?

In reality, both answers are true. When a person gets inspired to connect with Hashem, that inspiration is on a very high level, much higher than inspiration that comes from others. However, as we all know, self-generated inspiration can lack a level of commitment. As soon as the inspiration wanes, we go back to our old ways. So we need to prove to ourselves and to Hashem that we're serious. But once we overcome that challenge, then we see clearly how powerful our initial inspiration really was.

The same was true with Avraham Avinu. He doubtlessly experienced great spiritual inspiration in finding Hashem by himself, and for that Hashem could tell him to go on his mission immediately. However, until Avraham overcame this test, his true commitment would not be known.

This is a powerful point. Many times we have inspiration and it fades. When this happens, we often question ourselves. Were we really inspired...or not? The answer is: Of course we were inspired. However, to turn that inspiration into a reality, we must do something to prove it to Hashem and to ourselves. When we do this, we make our inspiration real, and connect to Hashem in the way that Avraham Avinu did.

· פרשת וירא ·

PARASHAS VAYEIRA

CHESED: A PILLAR OF LIFE

BY MOSHE PIANKO

Parashas Vayeira gives us a glimpse into the great acts of *chesed* that Avraham Avinu performed. Avraham Avinu always looked for the opportunity to do *hachnasas orchim*, even in the scorching heat on the third day after his bris, when the recovery was most painful. Once the chance to welcome guests presented itself, he ran to take care of them, involved his whole family in the mitzvah, gave them the choicest meat, and made sure they were comfortable.

The Mishnah in *Avos* (5:13) teaches that a tzaddik says, "What is mine is yours and what is yours is yours," whereas a *rasha* says, "What is yours in mine." Rabbi Shmuel Baron, *shlita*, recounted to me that his rebbe, Rabbi Avraham Yehoshua Soloveitchik, *shlita*, asked two questions on this mishnah. First, why would a person need to give away everything that is his in order to be considered a tzaddik? And second, why does the mishnah need to tell us that someone who treats everyone else's property as his own is a *rasha*? Isn't that obvious?

Rabbi Soloveitchik answers that the mishnah here is not simply describing the actions of a tzaddik and a *rasha*; rather, it is describing the worldview of the tzaddik and the *rasha*. The tzaddik always views his property as belonging to others, such that if there were ever an argument with another person over property, he would assume that the property in question must belong to the other person. By contrast, the *rasha* assumes everything belongs to him, so whenever he has an argument with another over property, he will assume the property must be his.

Rabbi Chaim Volozhiner interprets the Mishnah in a slightly different way. He understands it to mean that each person must see the world fundamentally as the place to do *chesed* for others—to believe that the entire world was created literally in order for each person to do *chesed* for another. Therefore, when it snowed in Volozhin, Rabbi Chaim would get up early in the morning before others awakened in order to be the one to shovel the snow on the path leading to the *beis midrash* so that the *bachurim* would be able to walk there easily. Thus, the Mishnah isn't telling us to simply give away our property to others. Instead, it is instructing us to use what we have in order to help others, and that the tzaddik sees everything he owns as a means for assisting his fellow man and is constantly acting accordingly.

Rabbi Eliyahu Eliezer Dessler, *zt"l*, in his famous *Kuntres Hachesed*, teaches that each person must fundamentally decide whether he wants to live his life as a giver or as a taker. He explains that loving someone, whether one's spouse or all Jews, leads to giving to that person, not to taking from him. That is the reason the *pasuk* in *Mishlei* (15:27) says, "*Sonei matanos yichyeh*—One who hates receiving gifts lives"; this person experiences the true essence of what life is about.

In these three explanations, we see how our *Gedolim* viewed the importance of *chesed*. *Chesed* isn't simply something that a person does; rather, it is a worldview, a way of life. By making *chesed* a part of our daily routine, we define ourselves as givers who love each and every Jew. We also demonstrate a deep understanding that this world was created specifically for us to give, such that with each act of giving, we realize our true *tafkid* in this world. In a way, we imitate Hashem, Who is the true Giver.

· פרשת חיי שרה ·

PARASHAS CHAYEI SARAH

ALL THE GOOD YEARS OF SARAH

BY RABBI ZVI KAMENETSKY

Immediately following *Akeidas Yitzchak*, at the end of *Parashas Vayeira*, our parashah begins with the passing of Sarah Imeinu. The opening *pasuk* details the number of years she lived and concludes: "*Shenei chayei Sarah*—The years of the life of Sarah" (*Bereishis* 23:1). Rashi comments on this phrase by quoting the words of our Sages: "*Kulan shavim letovah*—[Sarah's years] were all equally good." What is the significance of this observation?

The *Midrash Tanchuma* at the end of *Vayeira* explains the juxtaposition of the two events, *Akeidas Yitzchak* and the passing of Sarah, as follows: As far as we know, Sarah was unaware of the events leading up to *Akeidas Yitzchak*, as well as what transpired there. However, the Satan devised a scheme by which Sarah would first be told about the near loss of Yitzchak, which would cause her life-threatening anguish. Only then would she be made aware that Hashem commanded Avraham not to slaughter her son. However, before the Satan had the chance to finish the narrative, Sarah became so distressed that her "*neshamah* departed her." The sad reality, that Avraham and Yitzchak were not present when she passed away, is reflected at the beginning of *Parashas Chayei Sarah*: "*Vayavo Avraham lispod leSarah velivkosah*—And Avraham came to eulogize Sarah and cry over her" (*Bereishis* 23:2).

One of the most puzzling parts of this midrash is the reaction of Sarah to the *Akeidah*. After all, wasn't this meant to serve as a *nisayon* of Avraham's devotion and loyalty to the fulfillment of Hashem's will? If so, we would expect Sarah to have the ability to withstand and overcome her personal affection for Yitzchak by following the command of Hashem just as Avraham did. Yet, the blow Sarah received over this seemingly uncompromising submission to the will of Hashem was enough to cause her to die of shock. In *Parashas Vayeira*, we are told about the difference of opinion between Avraham and Sarah with regard to driving Yishmael out of their home. There, Hashem instructed Avraham: "*Kol asher tomar eilecha Sarah shema bekolah*—Whatever Sarah says to you, obey her voice" (ibid. 21:12). It is derived from here that Sarah was on an even higher level of *nevuah* than Avraham. We would assume, then, that she would have had the ability to withstand the emotional trauma of the fulfillment of the command of *Akeidas Yitzchak*. Why would hearing the news of the *Akeidah* cause her to die of shock?

The Ksav Sofer explains that there is no doubt Sarah would have agreed to and encouraged Avraham's following the command to sacrifice Yitzchak. What troubled her so much was her intense desire to have been tested in the same way that Avraham was. This missed opportunity bothered her to the extent that her *neshamah* left her.

This understanding can help to explain the end of the first *pasuk*. In case there were any skeptics who may have seen the passing of Sarah as a lacking in her loyalty to Hashem and fulfilling His will, the *pasuk* tells us, "*Kulan shavim letovah*," all of Sarah's days were consistent in her loyalty and devotion to Hashem. Her passing, in fact, was a result of the very same intense desire to connect with Hashem by fulfilling His will.

The one question that remains is: Why did Hashem leave Sarah out of this most challenging test? The Ksav Sofer explains: The word *nisayon* is rooted in the word *nes*, meaning a miracle or a banner which is held high for others to see. Hashem had no doubt that Avraham would pass the test. As the *Midrash Rabbah* explains, its purpose was to serve as a testament to why Avraham was deserving of Hashem's boundless love. This was displayed clearly, for all to see, in the unwavering love and fear of Hashem he displayed on Har Hamoriah. For Sarah, however, no such public display of loyalty was necessary. It was not of concern to the masses in the way that Hashem's relationship with Avraham was.

This explanation is very revealing regarding how such an incident can be interpreted in two completely opposite ways. On the one hand, we may interpret Sarah's heart-stopping reaction to the news of the *Akeidah* as a deficiency in her life's mission of demonstrating complete loyalty to the *ratzon Hashem*. However, in actuality, it was a sign of the strongest devotion to fulfilling His will.

There are times when we are faced with difficult *nisyonos*. These challenges sometimes wear us down, creating within our *neshamos* a feeling of despair. We begin to think that we are lacking in our *emunah*. However, the truth is just the opposite; in fact, it shows our unshakable belief in Hashem and the trust we have in His kindness. It is then that we must reinforce the foundations of our faith that have kept us going and have made us dependent on His protection and the unconditional kindness with which He created the universe.

· פרשת תולדות ·

PARASHAS TOLDOS

PRAYER: CONNECTING TO OUR FELLOW JEWS

BY HILLEL EFRON

At the beginning of *Parashas Toldos* we witness an often overlooked and amazing act of Yitzchak Avinu. It's an act of Divine power that we all too often attribute only to tzaddikim, a deed that may be too difficult for the average Jew. Yitzchak prayed on behalf of his wife to bear a child, and he was successful (*Bereishis* 25:21). Yitzchak's plea with Hashem was to reverse the nature of his wife's physical childbearing capabilities. How was he successful in this endeavor?

Rashi on this *pasuk* quotes the Gemara in *Yevamos* (64a) that Hashem answered Yitzchak's plea over Rivkah's because he was a *tzaddik ben tzaddik*, a righteous man the son of a righteous man, while Rivkah was a *tzaddik ben rasha*, a righteous woman who descended from a wicked man.

This explanation is difficult to understand. As we may imagine, the trials and tribulations that it took to overcome growing up in the house of a *rasha* should earn Rivkah some merit. She may very well have been a greater *tzadeikes* then Yitzchak. Furthermore, the Gemara in *Berachos* (34b) states that those who have repented and overcome adversity to draw close to Hashem are in much better standing, as it were, than those who have always been righteous: "As Rabbi Abahu said: In the place where penitents stand, even the full-fledged righteous do not stand, as it is stated: 'Peace, peace upon him who is far and him who is near.' Peace and greeting is extended first to him who is far, the penitent, and only thereafter is peace extended to him who is near, the full-fledged righteous one."

Would Rivkah not fit the bill as one who has been far and has come near? In comparison to Yitzchak, would she not be granted the blessing of peace before Hashem first? Would her pleas and prayers not carry more weight than Yitzchak's? What did he have that she did not?

I believe that Yitzchak's prayer skill set was the differentiator in this scenario. Praying is more than just the mere utterance of words, and prayer is more than just calling on the merit of righteous forbears. It is important to factor in an understanding of prayer and how to approach our needs and the needs of a fellow Jew.

This all started with the story of how Yitzchak was born. Earlier in *Bereishis* (ch. 20), the events of Avraham, Sarah, and Avimelech unfolded. To paraphrase, Avraham and Sarah came to the city of Gerar, and Avraham became fearful again that he may be killed in the efforts of the locals to take his wife, Sarah, for the king. Avraham told Sarah to convey their relationship as siblings and she appeared to comply. Avimelech, the local king, now had no need to eliminate Avraham, and he took Sarah to his house to be with her. That night, Avimelech and his household were afflicted with a terrible physical ailment. Hashem then came to him in a dream and told him about his wrongful taking of Sarah, commanded him to return her to her husband, and said, "Avraham will pray for your well-being." Avimelech did everything that Hashem commanded of him. There was then an exchange of words and gifts, and Avraham prayed for Avimelech.

The following three *pesukim* unveil for us the skill set for prayer. However, before we proceed, we must understand that the success of one's prayers is measured not by their fulfillment but by the transformation of the one praying. As our Sages describe in many places, prayer is a substitute for the service in the Beis Hamikdash. This service primarily consisted of *korbanos*. The word *korban* comes from the root word *karov*, meaning in close proximity. The goal of the Temple service was to connect and come close to Hashem. Thus, our prayer has become the *avodah shebalev*, the service that's in our hearts. It is a way to connect to Hashem, or maybe even to other Jews, via the attributes of the heart.

Let's continue to examine the prayers of Avraham for Avimelech (ibid. 20:17–18, 21:1):

וַיִּתְפַּלֵּל אַבְרָהָם אֶל הָאֱלֹהִים וַיִּרְפָּא אֱלֹהִים אֶת אֲבִימֶלֶךְ וְאֶת אִשְׁתּוֹ וְאַמְהֹתָיו וַיֵּלֵדוּ. כִּי עָצֹר עָצַר ה' בְּעַד כָּל רֶחֶם לְבֵית אֲבִימֶלֶךְ עַל דְּבַר שָׂרָה אֵשֶׁת אַבְרָהָם. וַה' פָּקַד אֶת שָׂרָה כַּאֲשֶׁר אָמָר וַיַּעַשׂ ה' לְשָׂרָה כַּאֲשֶׁר דִּבֵּר.

Avraham then prayed to Hashem, and Hashem healed Avimelech and his wife and his slave girls, so that they bore children. For Hashem had closed fast every womb of the household of Avimelech because of Sarah, the wife of Avraham... Hashem took note of Sarah as He had promised, and Hashem did for Sarah as He had spoken.

Rashi points out the juxtaposition of Avraham's prayers for the closed wombs of the household of Avimelech and the promise made to Sarah to bear a child. He directs us to the Gemara in *Bava Kamma* (92a):

Rava said to Rabba bar Mari: From where is this matter derived whereby the Sages stated: "Anyone who asks for compassion from Heaven on behalf of another, and he requires compassion from Heaven concerning that same matter, he is answered first"?

The Gemara then answers by citing Avraham's prayer for Avimelech as the source of this Divine reality.

The commentaries on how exactly this works are numerous. But the most profound message is in the simplicity of our Sages' words. It's not just about praying for someone else; it's about praying for someone else who has the very same needs as you—praying for someone who is in need of the same Heavenly compassion. To pray wholeheartedly means taking one's own painful feelings of desperation and transforming them to feel for another and truly share a common pain. Avraham used his own experience to help him feel the pain of Avimelech and his household, the pain of being childless. This virtue of prayer, the skill of connecting to another through a common need or a common pain is, by its own definition, a successful prayer.

The goal of prayer is to connect to Hashem and come closer to Him, just as a *korban* would do. During troubling times, Hashem is not merely watching. He is with us, partaking in the pain. When we hurt, He hurts. When we cry, He cries. And as with everything, we are at our best when we emulate the Divine attributes and carry our friend's burden.

Reexamining our original questions, we see why Yitzchak was successful in his prayers and why his were answered over Rivkah's. A tzaddik is a person who has the ability to connect with others, to feel and share in another's pain. And Yitzchak was taught this attribute from childhood, since he was, as it were, birthed from this attribute. Rivkah did not grow up in a house where one's inner pain was used to connect with and share in another's pain. Most probably the opposite was true, where inner pain was turned into hate, greed, and anger.

In fact, this point becomes clear if we look at the *pasuk* again (*Bereishis* 25:21).

וַיֶּעְתַּר יִצְחָק לַה' לְנֹכַח אִשְׁתּוֹ כִּי עֲקָרָה הִוא וַיֵּעָתֶר לוֹ ה' וַתַּהַר רִבְקָה אִשְׁתּוֹ.

Yitzchak pleaded with Hashem on behalf of his wife because she was barren; and Hashem responded to his plea, and his wife Rivkah conceived.

In the first part of the *pasuk*, Yitzchak's prayer refers to his relationship to *ishto*, his wife, and her distress. In Hashem's answer, the Torah refers to Rivkah by name. It is highlighting that Yitzchak used the skill of connection through mutual pain to plead on her behalf.

Unfortunately, there is no shortage of *tzaros* for us to pray for. Almost everyone has had an encounter with personal loss, illness, or a desperate situation. This gives us the tremendous opportunity to share in each other's pain. When we approach prayer, let's take a moment to reflect on our own personal difficulties. Bring up the emotion and sit with the pain. Know that your fellow Jew has pain as well. This is the starting point of prayer. This is what is meant by the aforementioned phrase *avodah shebalev*, the service in our hearts, that describes prayer so accurately. This was the skill of Avraham and Yitzchak, and it is available to everyone.

· פרשת ויצא ·

PARASHAS VAYEITZEI

HASHAKAH AND NESHIKAH

BY MEIR MONDROW

Prior to Yaakov meeting his future wife Rachel, the Torah relates an incident where he encountered a gathering of shepherds waiting to uncover a well to give water to their flocks. In this brief episode, different forms of the word *hashakah*, to give a drink, appear five times in a nine-*pasuk* span (see *Bereishis* 29:2–10). Then, when Yaakov met Rachel, the parashah continues with appearances of the cognate *neshikah*, kissing, in two out of the next three *pesukim*. For added measure, one can take notice of the seemingly extraneous usage of the words *pi habe'eir*, mouth of the well—apparently related to *neshikah/hashakah*—in the aforementioned *pesukim*.

What can account for this pattern embedded in the passage?

The Ramban (*Bereishis* 29:2) illuminates the way:

> According to our Sages in *Bereishis Rabbah*, there is a secret hint to the future here... In order to tell him [Yaakov] that he would be successful on his journey and he would merit to have children, he merited this hint, because the well alludes to the Beis Hamikdash, and the three shepherds symbolize the three times a year the Jewish people come to the Beis Hamikdash, because the well is what the shepherds will use to water the flock, as from there they will be able to draw out *ruach hakodesh*.

When one draws from a well, he is accessing the most basic life-sustaining element, water, from a somewhat hidden source, and allowing for it to be imbibed into oneself. The well here represents the Beis

Hamikdash, the source of spirituality—seemingly hidden—and the *ha-shakah* of water represents the *ruach hakodesh*, the most sublime spirituality, which we draw from there. The deeper message of this episode lies in how it serves as a harbinger for the ultimate goal of Yaakov's progeny: the Beis Hamikdash experience. *Hashakah*, the reception of this spirituality, is central to that experience.

But how does this explanation of *hashakah* connect to *neshikah*?

When Moshe Rabbeinu encountered Aharon upon returning from Midian, the Torah records that one brother kissed the other. Rabbi Shlomo Ashtruc (*Midreshei HaTorah, Bereishis* 29:11) comments:[4]

> There is no indication who kissed whom. The intention is that each one influenced the other. This is similar to what is written, "*Yishakeini mineshikos pihu*—May He kiss me with kisses of the mouth" (*Shir Hashirim* 1:2) because the kissing that is written regarding tzaddikim connotes an abundance of spiritual bounty.

Rabbi Ashtruc explains that the *neshikah* of tzaddikim is *atzilus shefa*, a flowing from what's internal for them to others. It connotes the impact they make on other people.

Rabbi Shlomo Alkabetz takes this a step further.[5] He explains that the *neshikah* of tzaddikim is bidirectional, not only concerning drawing from what is hidden within and bequeathing to others, but also allowing the one being influenced to rise up toward the one influencing him.

---

4. I thank Rabbi Reuven Chaim Klein of Beitar Illit in Eretz Yisrael for providing the sources which follow from Rabbi Shlomo Ashtruc and Rabbi Shlomo Alkabetz in the main text, and the midrashim of footnote 2, as well as the comments of Rabbi Chaim Paltiel in footnote 3. For further elaboration on all matters related to *neshikah*, see Rabbi Klein's exhaustive study of the topic in the journal *Chitzei Gibborim, Peleitas Sofrim*, booklet 8 (*Elul* 5775): 675–86.

5. *Shoresh Yishai* to *Rus* 1:15, also quoted in *Anaf Yosef* to *Midrash Tanchuma, Shemos, siman* 26, and *Eitz Yosef* to *Rus Rabbah* 2:21, both in the name of *Iggeres Shmuel*, who in turn quotes Rabbi Alkabetz.

All this—as per the aforementioned comments of the Ramban—converges in the Beis Hamikdash, the place where "the earth and heaven kiss each other" (*Bava Basra* 74a),[6] and this is perhaps what the Torah was emphasizing when it used these two words so often during this episode.[7]

While the basic form of the concept has been outlined, we may also draw something practical from what has been delineated. When we have the privilege and pleasure of kissing our loved ones, we should at times reflect on the profound depth of what this action accomplishes. We are at once giving from the deepest recesses and most sublime essence of ourselves, and simultaneously raising up the recipient of our affection in the hopes of their attaining the best of what we have to offer.

It is of no coincidence that the aforementioned *pasuk* relates, "*Yishakeini mineshikos pihu*—May He kiss me with kisses of the mouth" (*Shir Hashirim* 1:2), using kissing as a *mashal* for our love of Hashem. The implication of this concept is that our intense love of our relatives is similar to the love we have for Hashem. Both are based on a heartfelt emotional attachment, of giving of ourselves and our essence, to express the deepest of bonds.

---

6. Explained in accordance with the Malbim in *HaTorah Vehamitzvah* to *Bereishis* 28:17. It is worthwhile to also take note of Rabbi Chaim Paltiel's comments to *Bereishis* 29:11:

וַיִּשַּׁק יַעֲקֹב לְרָחֵל. תֵּמַהּ הוּא שֶׁנּוֹשֵׁק אִשָּׁה שֶׁלֹּא רָאָה מִיָּמָיו, וְעוֹד שֶׁבָּכָה וְאֵין נְשִׁיקָה ע"י בְּכִיָּה. לָכֵן י"ל שֶׁהוּא כְּמוֹ 'וְאַל אִישֵׁךְ תְּשׁוּקָתֵךְ' (בראשית ג, טז). ועי"ל שֶׁהָיָה תָּאֵב לָקַח אוֹתָהּ שֶׁרָאָה שֶׁיִּהְיֶה לָהּ בָּנִים שֶׁבְּחֶלְקָם יָבָּנֶה בֵּית הַמְּקְדָּשׁ.

7. Lavan's kissing is, of course, not one of *hashpa'ah*, but rather the opposite—see Rashi's comments to *Bereishis* 29:13; Lavan was essentially accosting Yaakov in the hope of obtaining valuables. Nonetheless, the appearance of his *neshikah* underscores the general theme.

· פרשת וישלח ·

PARASHAS VAYISHLACH

THE PROHIBITION AGAINST EATING THE GID HANASHEH

BY ELI SHICKER

Adapted from a derashah given by Rabbi Y. Y. Jacobson on TheYeshiva.net.

One of the most mysterious events to occur in *Sefer Bereishis*, and perhaps in the entire Torah, is when Yaakov was left alone and wrestled with an *ish*, a man (*Bereishis* 32:25). The Torah does not say who the man was, but the most common explanation comes from Rashi, who points out that our Sages teach us that he was Eisav's guardian angel.

This peculiar event took place after Yaakov sent gifts of livestock in the hope of appeasing Eisav before they met. Then Yaakov gathered his family, and they were the first to cross the river Yabok. But Yaakov did not cross with them; rather, he sent his family ahead and stayed alone, where he was attacked by the aforementioned *ish*.

Realizing that he would not emerge victorious against Yaakov, the angel injured Yaakov in his thigh. Before Yaakov left, he asked the angel for a blessing. The angel asked Yaakov what his name was, and after Yaakov responded, the angel said that from now on Yaakov would be known as Yisrael, for he had striven with Hashem and with man and prevailed. To make this incident even more bizarre, the episode ends with a commandment not to eat the *gid hanasheh*, the sciatic nerve found in a kosher animal's thigh, because that was where the angel injured Yaakov.

The obscurity of this event and the mitzvah that follows begs the question: Why does the Torah memorialize this ostensibly minor, isolated event of a random middle-of-the-night wrestling match?

It is important to note that the Torah does not share a specific event unless that very event has further meaning. The fact that this episode was detailed in such a way means there is a much deeper and significant lesson than what appears on the surface. There are some commentaries who say the reason for the prohibition of *gid hanasheh* is to teach a lesson in *kibbud av va'eim*: Yaakov's children should not have left their father alone, for this directly led to his injury. Therefore, Yaakov's descendants took it upon themselves not to eat this nerve that was injured as a reminder to children not to leave their parents alone.

Most commentators, however, delve deeper into what happened between Yaakov and the angel and uncover a timelessly pertinent lesson for the Jewish people. The struggle between Yaakov and the angel symbolizes the plight and the history of the Jewish people for thousands of years to come. It was specifically after this event that Yaakov's name was changed to Yisrael—representing the entire Jewish nation. This hints to the fact that what appeared to be a personal struggle for Yaakov had future implications for the entirety of Bnei Yisrael. Just as Yaakov was randomly attacked in the middle of the night in a seemingly unprovoked assault, so too there will be people and governments in every generation that will indiscriminately hate the Jewish people and try to annihilate them. But just like the angel was unable to kill Yaakov, the Jewish people will never be destroyed, and they'll continue to persevere. Like Yaakov, the Jewish people will get wounded, sometimes gravely, with enduring pain and suffering, but they will ultimately prevail.

If this incident represents in fact a microcosm of the history of the Jewish people, then the prohibition against eating the *gid hanasheh* seems like a strange way to commemorate such a monumental event. The existence of Yaakov—and the Jewish people—was threatened, yet he survived, and the way in which his descendants remember this occurrence is by not eating a small nerve of an animal because it reflects where Yaakov was injured? The Jewish people have struggled many times throughout history, and the way in which we celebrate is with holidays and mitzvos directly related to the momentous event. On Purim, we celebrate our survival with reading the Megillah, eating a celebratory feast, and performing several other mitzvos associated with the story. We memorialize our victory over the Greeks with eight nights of Chanukah, when we light candles, eat special foods, and play dreidel. To remind us of our freedom on Pesach, we conduct a Seder, during which we tell the story of our slavery and eventual redemption from Egypt, while eating special foods as reminders of that time, like matzah and *maror*.

But here there is no celebratory feast or retelling of the story of when Yaakov's life was spared. Instead, the Torah informs generations to come of a prohibition against eating a tiny part of an animal. Why not celebrate the bigger picture of the Jewish people's continued existence instead of focusing on such a minor, negligible detail? In other words, how is the prohibition of *gid hanasheh* representative of Bnei Yisrael's unrelenting survival and existence?

The fact that the Torah hones in on this seemingly small detail teaches an important and powerful lesson in *hashgachah pratis*. The history of the Jewish people, as well as the entire world, is not just about what occurs during the well-known, dramatic events. Rather, even the small, seemingly insignificant details that happen daily to individuals are a part of Hashem's providence.

The Ba'al Shem Tov revolutionized this idea of *hashgachah pratis*. He taught that Hashem involves Himself not only in major world events that determine the survival of a people, such as a world war or a global pandemic. Hashem didn't just create the laws of nature and then let the world run itself with random occurrences that are generated by those forces. Instead, even the most seemingly mundane occurrence, such as the wind blowing or an animal dying, is part of Hashem's providence. On a personal level, this means that something as trivial as scraping one's knee is an expression of Hashem's *hashgachah pratis*.

The Torah could have focused on the bigger picture of Yaakov and the Jewish people emerging victorious, and commanded Bnei Yisrael to celebrate with feasting and public festivities. But instead, we memorialize this event by focusing on the "minor" detail, the sciatic nerve, which is less than an inch in diameter, because it represents the belief that even the seemingly insignificant details are part of Hashem's plan.

May we all be blessed to see the details of our lives as part of a bigger picture of Hashem's ultimate *hashgachah pratis*.

· פרשת וישב ·

PARASHAS VAYEISHEV

HASHEM'S PLAN IS ALWAYS PRECISE

BY YONA BILDNER

Toward the beginning of *Parashas Vayeishev*, Yaakov asked Yosef to go to his brothers, who were tending sheep in Shechem, see how they were, and report back. Rabbi Samson Raphael Hirsch explains that Yaakov could sense a rift between Yosef and his brothers. He therefore sent Yosef to be together with them, in the hope of repairing the rift. However, the Torah tells us that Yosef met a seemingly random person on the journey, who informed him that his brothers had, in fact, moved on from Shechem to Dosan.

Why would the brothers depart for Dosan? The sequence of events makes it appear that they were running away from something. My understanding is that the brothers were trying to further throw Yosef off their scent. They knew that would Yosef come to them, they would kill him. By traveling to Dosan, the brothers gave themselves just enough time for their intense hatred and jealousy to wane so that they were open to accepting Yehudah's suggestion to sell Yosef instead of killing him.

What was the purpose of this whole scenario? Why were the brothers in Shechem, the town that Shimon and Levi had destroyed, in the first place? Could they not tend sheep elsewhere? The Radak explains that they put their trust in Hashem, Who had caused the inhabitants to fear them before. I would surmise that initially, they wanted to be away from Yosef. Shechem, a city in which their family was surely hated, would be the last place Yosef would look for them. Yosef found out where they had gone only through Yaakov, whom the brothers had apparently informed regarding their location.

When they realized Yosef was coming, the brothers moved to Dosan. Each segment had to have been perfectly timed. Sufficient time was needed for the brothers to be flexible enough to accept sentencing their brother to slavery and not death, yet not so much that they would come to their senses and decide not to respond at all.

Rabbeinu Bachya explains that Yaakov is referred to as Yisrael in this story (*Bereishis* 37:13), in order to "reflect his higher spiritual nature as the architect of national destiny." Similarly, we can compare this story to the tale of Yonah and the whale. Yonah attempted to run away from his duty, but in the end destiny prevailed. The brothers tried to escape what they knew was coming, but in the end Hashem's plan played out with perfect precision—as it always does.

· פרשת מקץ ·

PARASHAS MIKEITZ

REALIZING THE REASONS
FOR OUR SUCCESS

BY RABBI EPHRAIM MESSING

At the end of *Parashas Vayeishev*, Yosef successfully interpreted the dream of the *sar hamashkim*, predicting his reinstatement in the palace. However, despite Yosef's request for the *sar hamashkim* to return the favor by putting in a good word to Pharaoh, the *sar hamashkim* "did not remember Yosef and forgot him" (*Bereishis* 40:23).

Rashi comments that because Yosef placed his faith in the *sar hamashkim* rather than in Hashem, he needed to wait another two years before being released from prison, a fact that the Torah makes sure to inform us of as we begin *Parashas Mikeitz* ("And it was at the end of two years" [ibid. 41:1]). The obvious question that arises is, what about *hishtadlus*? Why is it a contradiction to trust in Hashem while making the reasonable effort required to get oneself out of a predicament? Aren't we *not* supposed to rely on miracles?

Rabbi Lord Jonathan Sacks, *zt"l*, points out something interesting about Yosef's life. Until this point, Yosef had been completely at the mercy of external forces. He'd been consistently acted upon (by his father and brothers, the stranger in the field, the traveling merchants, Potiphar and his wife) rather than acting upon others. Even the things he did manage to do on his own were explicitly attributed to Hashem: "Hashem blessed the Egyptian because of Yosef" (ibid. 39:5); "Hashem was with Yosef, and He showed him kindness, making him find favor with the warden" (ibid. 39:21); "Hashem was with him, and Hashem granted him success in everything he did" (ibid. 39:3). When it came to dreams, Yosef said it was not his wisdom but Hashem's that provided the interpretation (ibid. 40:8). When he resisted Potiphar's wife's advances, he said, "How could I do such a thing before Hashem?" (ibid. 39:9).

Only now does the theme shift. For the first time, Yosef asserted himself and tried taking matters into his own hands—and he failed. At least that's how it seemed during those long two years he languished in prison. And that was for a reason. Because, as it had been all along, it was not Yosef's plans and efforts that got him released; it was Hashem's will that intervened. Had he been released immediately, he would not have learned this vital lesson, one he would need as he began to move in earnest into the realm of political, pragmatic activity. This was a lesson he'd relay to his own brothers upon revealing himself to them: "You did not send me here; Hashem did, and He made me…a powerful ruler over all of Egypt" (ibid. 45:8).

Had Yosef simply continued being acted upon, passively subjected to one tribulation after another, or gone from one clearly Divinely assisted success to the next, he wouldn't have learned the balance he would need to succeed as viceroy. For when he came out of his prison he was no longer the same passive, humble Yosef. He knew his abilities and made every effort to apply himself, so as to save the land and ultimately his family from famine. Had he remained passive, or reliant on providential assistance, he wouldn't have achieved what he did, and wouldn't have been able to attribute even such great success to Hashem. He needed to absorb the hard lesson he learned in the depths of the dungeon, to know and understand that even when he asserted himself and had success doing so, it was still Hashem running the show.

In life, great achievements require genuine effort and talent, which Yosef possessed and applied in abundance. We're not supposed to be passive in this world. That wouldn't reveal Hashem's greatness. He expects us to put in our effort, apply our talent, and, despite it all, to recognize that the results are ultimately not in our control. All we can do is our part, and be grateful for what we are given, what we can see and understand, and know it's all in Hashem's hands, and all for a reason.

That's the lesson Yosef learned, the lesson only he could share with his brothers, and ultimately with us.

· פרשת ויגש ·

PARASHAS VAYIGASH

WALKING BY FAITH, NOT BY SIGHT

BY JOEY SMALL

It may be one of the most dramatic encounters in *Sefer Bereishis*. An encounter that had probably played out many times in each participant's mind. An encounter that was full of mixed emotions and unanswered questions. This critical meeting was the moment Yaakov reunited with his son Yosef after twenty-two years.

In describing when Yaakov and Yosef saw each other after all those years, the Torah tells us, "And Yosef prepared his chariot and went up to greet his father, Yisrael, in Goshen. He [Yosef] saw him and fell on the neck of his father and cried" (*Bereishis* 46:29). Rashi comments that while Yosef was crying on the neck of his father, Yaakov was reciting *Kerias Shema*. After twenty-two years of mourning for his son, Yaakov is not recorded in the Torah as crying in his first embrace with his son or showering him with kisses and warm greetings; rather, while his son emotionally embraced him with tears in his eyes, Yaakov recited the Shema. Why was Yaakov saying Shema, and why was he the *only* one saying Shema?

Many *meforshim* write that this was the happiest moment in Yaakov's life. It was the moment when he realized that he was worthy to be the father of the *shevatim*, and that Yosef, his *ben zekunim*, would be able to continue transmitting the values he had inherited from his parents. When Yaakov saw Yosef as a religiously committed Jew who rose to the highest ranks in Egypt, he saw the culmination of many years of hoping that Yaakov would merit to father the twelve tribes of Israel. And when a tzaddik feels a great love in his heart, he channels those feelings toward Hashem. It was at this happiest of moments that

Yaakov wanted to acknowledge Hashem as the singular driving force in the world. Therefore, he recited the Shema.

As this scenario played out, it became evident that Yaakov was utilizing the momentous occasion to remind himself, and perhaps teach his son, of one of life's most important lessons as a Jew: to believe that Hashem has a master plan. When Pharaoh asked him, "How many are the days of the years of your life?" Yaakov answered, "Few and bad have been the years of my life" (ibid. 47:8–9). Yaakov described his own life as one of struggle, uncertainty, and sadness. But when he got a glimpse of Hashem's plan and understood for an instant how his prior struggles were designed to bring him to that moment and actualize the dream of a Jewish nation, his natural response was to say the Shema.

Whispering to himself (but perhaps hoping that his son was listening as well), Yaakov said, "Listen, Yisrael (another name for himself), Hashem is our God, Hashem is One." He was telling himself and all of Bnei Yisrael that Hashem loves us and has a plan for ourselves that is larger than we can possibly understand. And when Yaakov experienced this moment of recognizing that there are no contradictions in Hashem's actions and that everything He does is a step toward the fulfillment of His plan, his emotional well surged. It became easier to grasp the vicissitudes of his life. At that moment, he realized and accepted that everything Hashem does has a purpose and is part of His one plan.

Recognizing the Oneness of Hashem in all of life's experiences is not an easy task. In fact, a mortal, finite human being can never understand or comprehend an infinite being. Perhaps that's another reason why we cover our eyes every time we recite the *pasuk* that Yaakov said on the very day he met his son after twenty-two years. Beyond just helping us concentrate, placing our hands over our eyes symbolizes that even though we can't see Hashem's plan, we do our best to believe in it.

That is the true lesson of the Shema. It's an acknowledgment that even if we do not understand how an event in our lives is part of Hashem's plan, the message is that Hashem and Elokeinu are both One. When glimpses of that Oneness are perceived at any level, that can lead to a great sense of love for Hashem. After all, the *gematria* of the word *echad* equals that of *ahavah*; we see that part of our love for Hashem emanates from our recognition of His Oneness in the world. In fact, in both *Shacharis* and *Ma'ariv*, the text of the Shema is sandwiched between a verse detailing Hashem's love for us ("*habocheir be'amo Yisrael be'ahavah*" in the morning and "*oheiv es amo Yisrael be'ahavah*" in the evening) and another detailing our obligation to love Him back ("*ve'ahavta es Hashem Elokecha*").

When we accept that Hashem loves us unconditionally and that everything He does comes from a place of love, it makes it more understandable that everything we experience comes from *Hashem Echad*. As we pledge our allegiance to Hashem every day with the recitation of the Shema, we remind ourselves of the moment Yaakov recognized the Oneness of Hashem's plan. Rabbi Gedalia Schorr, *zt"l*, says that in the same way that a single ray of light disperses into a rainbow of colors when it hits a prism, so too, Hashem's Oneness is perceived by different people in a variety of ways on this earth. However, when cover our eyes with our hands, we remind ourselves that while it really is impossible for us to see Hashem's one plan in totality, we must still believe it.

· פרשת ויחי ·

PARASHAS VAYECHI

FUTURE CLARITY

BY DANNY GOTTESMAN

In the first *pasuk* of *Parashas Vayechi*, the Torah states that Yaakov lived in the land of Egypt for seventeen years and "*vayehi yemei Yaakov shenei chayav*—the days of Yaakov, the years of his life" were 147 years (*Bereishis* 47:28).

In his *sefer Ma'ayan Beis Hasho'eivah*, Rabbi Shimon Schwab, *zt"l*, points out that grammatically, the Torah should have said *vayehiyu* in the plural, not *vayehi* in the singular, as the word is modifying the days of Yaakov's life.

To resolve this question, Rabbi Schwab quotes from Rabbi Samson Raphael Hirsch in *Parashas Vayigash* (*Bereishis* 47:9), who explains as follows. When Pharaoh asked Yaakov how old he was, Yaakov responded, "*Yemei shenei megurai*—The days of the years of my sojourns" have been 130 years, and the "*yemei shenei chayai*—the days of the years of my lives" have been few and bad and have not reached the life spans of my forefathers in the days of their sojourns. There, Yaakov contrasted his life—in which he sojourned for 130 years but the actual positive days of his life were few—with the lives of his forefathers, in which their sojourns in this world were equal to the days of their lives (i.e., they were all positive in nature).

Yaakov encountered challenges throughout his life. When he finally overcame the difficulties of Eisav, Lavan, and Dinah, during which he certainly did not experience *yemei chaim* and live in tranquility, he was immediately presented with a new, more horrifying test: Yosef's disappearance.

However, once Yaakov had an opportunity to settle in Egypt for the final seventeen years of his life, and the *shevatim* were at peace and learning Torah in his *beis midrash*, those seventeen years became *yemei shenei chayav*. Those days were *mei'ein Olam Haba*. Just as in Olam Haba the tzaddikim are able to sense and understand that even the bad things that happened to them were for the good, so too here, Yaakov was able to understand that all of the challenges he encountered were for the good. As the Gemara (*Pesachim* 50a) states, in this world, one can only say "*baruch Dayan Ha'emes*" (blessed is the True Judge) upon hearing bad news, but in the next world, it is "*kulo hatov vehameitiv*" (everything is the One Who is good and bestows good).

During those seventeen years, Yaakov Avinu was able to perceive what tzaddikim are generally able to sense only in Olam Haba. Thus, the *pasuk* states that the "days of Yaakov," which initially seemed to be bad and just days of sojourns, "*vayehi*" were retroactively transformed into *shenei chayav*, the positive years of his life.

Along the same lines, Rabbi Asher Weiss, *shlita*, quotes from the Sanzer Rebbe, *zt"l*, who states that this is the reason we cover our eyes when we accept the yoke of Heaven while saying Shema. In the *pasuk* of *Shema Yisrael*, we say, "*Hashem Elokeinu Hashem Echad.*" We know that the Name Hashem refers to Hashem's *middas harachamim*, while the Name Elokim refers to His *middas hadin*. When we say the Shema, we declare that these Names of Hashem are really one, and the *middas hadin* is incorporated in the *middas harachamim*; we just cannot see this in Olam Hazeh. Therefore we cover our eyes. So while intellectually we can state that "*kol d'avid Rachmana letav avid*—everything that Hashem does is for the best," we cannot see it at this time.

May we all merit to be given the clarity and understanding that all of the challenges and suffering that Klal Yisrael has experienced, both on national and individual levels, were truly *letav*, for good, with the coming of Mashiach speedily in our days.

· פרשת שמות ·

PARASHAS SHEMOS

HAVING FAITH IN THE JEWISH PEOPLE

BY RABBI DANIEL ROSENFELD

When Hashem first approached Moshe Rabbeinu and tasked him with the mission of returning to Egypt to demand the release of the Jewish people, Moshe responded with intense ambivalence. His humility simply didn't allow him to realize that he was a worthy choice for such a lofty task, and only after much coaxing did he finally agree. In the middle of this back-and-forth between Moshe Rabbeinu and Hashem, Moshe suggested that there was no point in him going on such a mission, since "they won't believe me, and they won't listen to my voice, since they will say that Hashem did not appear to me" (*Shemos* 4:1). Immediately afterward, Hashem began giving Moshe a series of miracles to perform before the Jewish people to convince them to believe him, beginning with turning his staff into a snake.

Commenting on this *pasuk*, the *Midrash Rabbah* (3:12, see also Rashi there, who references the midrash briefly), suggests that this first sign was actually a veiled criticism against Moshe, as his suggestion that the Jewish people wouldn't believe him reflected a certain lack of *emunah* in Hashem (Who had already informed Moshe that they would believe him), and a lack of *emunah* in the Jews themselves, who are *ma'aminim bnei ma'aminim*, believers the children of believers. Therefore, Hashem presented to him the miracle of turning a staff into a snake, a reference to the original snake, who also used his speech to be critical of Hashem in Gan Eden when trying to convince Chavah to sin (*Bereishis* 3:5).

The Jewish people, despite the intense suffering of the enslavement, were still yearning for redemption, both physical and spiritual, and did not give in to cynicism or despair. Surely there were times when such feelings arose, but at their core, Bnei Yisrael's connection with Hashem and *emunah* in Him and the redemption never disappeared.

This idea of having *emunah* in the Jewish people as a whole relates to a discussion by Rabbi Yosef Dov Soloveitchik, *zt"l*, in *Al Hateshuvah* (pp. 93–98) regarding the fundamental *machlokes* between Rabbi Yehoshua and Rabbi Eliezer in *Sanhedrin* 97b about the ultimate redemption: According to Rabbi Yehoshua, the redemption is not dependent on *teshuvah*; rather, when the appointed time comes, Hashem will redeem us, irrespective of our spiritual state at that time. By contrast, according to Rabbi Eliezer, the redemption depends on *teshuvah*; it will come only when we are on the spiritual level to deserve it. The Rambam (*Mishneh Torah, Hilchos Teshuvah* 7:5) accepts the opinion of Rabbi Eliezer.8 This means that our ultimate redemption has no due date; it is completely in our hands.

But if that is the case, how could one of the statements in *Ani Ma'amin*, the thirteen pillars of faith enumerated by the Rambam, be that we wait each day for the imminent redemption? Rabbi Soloveitchik explains, based on the formulation of the Rambam there, that our *emunah* in the coming of Mashiach is in actuality *emunah* in the Jewish people themselves. No matter how far we stray, and no matter how many mistakes we make, each and every one of us is truly pure, good, and connected to Hashem, and will therefore certainly come back to Him at some point.

May we be *zocheh* to have *emunah* in our own potential, and in the potential of our fellow Jews, and through that achieve the ultimate *geulah*, speedily in our days.

---

8. This also appears to be the opinion of the Ramban; see the Ramban on *Vayikra* 26:16.

· פרשת וארא ·

PARASHAS VA'EIRA

THE MANY NAMES OF ḤASHEM

BY RABBI MATAN WEXLER

At the beginning of *Parashas Va'eira* (*Shemos* 6:3), Hashem told Moshe that He had appeared to Avraham, Yitzchak, and Yaakov as א-ל ש-ד-י, Keil Sha-kai, the "all-sufficing God," but had not become known to them as יקוק, the Tetragrammaton, often referred to as "Hashem." Although these words were directed specifically to Moshe, they carry a message for each and every one of us as well.

In order to unpack this message, the purpose of a name, and the usage of the particular Names of Hashem found in this *pasuk*, need to be explained. In general, a name provides context, and in so doing enables others to better understand, relate to, and connect to that which is named. This is a connection between the Hebrew word *shem* (שם), name, and *sham* (שם), there, which share the same letters. With this background, let us focus on the particular Names of Hashem highlighted in the *pasuk* above.

Rabbi Samson Raphael Hirsch, in his commentary on *Bereishis* 2:4, expands upon the words of our Sages, that the Tetragrammaton symbolizes Hashem's *middas harachamim*, adding that this Name signifies "His rule in history." In other words, a person may become fully aware of Hashem's mercy only after "seeing" His involvement in the totality of the history of the world. As such, Rabbi Hirsch (*Shemos* 6:3) suggests, this is why only after the ultimate *geulah* will Hashem's Name be known: "*Lachein yeida ami shemi*—My nation will know My Name" (*Yeshayahu* 52:6).

Elsewhere (*Bereishis* 17:1), Rabbi Hirsch examines the nature of the Name Keil Sha-kai, where he offers two approaches. We will focus on his first approach. He suggests that the etymology of the Name Sha-kai is rooted in the word *dai*, enough. This Name carries the twin message that "I am the One Who said: 'Enough!'" and "It is enough for the world that I am its God." When Hashem created the world, He set limits to His own creations' understanding of this world. It is enough for His creations to know only that Hashem is God, without understanding His ways. It seems that this Name of Hashem evokes the sense that we have a limited understanding of how He runs the world. This is also the Name that Hashem used to introduce His command to Avraham to "walk" before Hashem and become *tamim*, complete (ibid.).

Rabbi Hirsch explains here (*Shemos* 6:3) that Hashem guided the *Avos* through difficult and tumultuous experiences, and interacted with them in a restrained manner, as Keil Sha-kai, the all-sufficing God; the *Avos* never knew Hashem as expressed by the Tetragrammaton. It wasn't that the *Avos* weren't aware of the Tetragrammaton as a Name of Hashem; rather, they never actually saw Him operate this way during their lifetimes.

At the end of *Parashas Shemos*, Moshe got a taste of the way Hashem related to the *Avos* when, not only was he met with rejection by Pharaoh and the Jewish people, but he seemed to make matters worse for the Jews. At that point, he exclaimed to Hashem, "*Heira la'am hazeh vehatzeil lo hitzalta es amecha*—He [Pharaoh] has abused the people even more, and You have not rescued Your people even from this?!" (ibid. 5:23), to which Hashem responded, "*Atah sireh*—Now you will see" (ibid. 6:1). Moshe would now be given the privilege of gaining a historical perspective on Hashem, where he would literally see the redemption of Bnei Yisrael. At the beginning of *Parashas Va'eira*, Hashem communicated this message to Moshe by contrasting the lives of the *Avos* to his own experience.

We haven't yet been privileged to personally experience Hashem's involvement in our lives and the world at-large as expressed in the Tetragrammaton. If anything, at most we can relate to the Keil Sha-kai experience of our *Avos*.

Perhaps that is why we begin the *Shemoneh Esrei* by describing

Hashem as the God of our *Avos* and not the God of Moshe. We are capable of praising Hashem through the lens of knowing Him as Keil Sha-kai, but not as the Tetragrammaton (see Rabbi Hirsch's reference to *Yeshayahu* 52:6 above). In fact, contained within the opening declaration of "the God of Avraham, the God of Yitzchak, and the God of Yaakov" is the message that each of us must uniquely come to our own belief in Hashem, as each of our *Avos* independently cultivated their own *emunah* in Him (see the *Eitz Yosef* commentary on the siddur).

The principle of *ma'aseh avos siman labanim*, the deeds of the forefathers serve as a guide for the children, is as true today as ever before. It's not merely that the actions of our ancestors foreshadow what the Jewish nation as a whole will experience; it's also that the lives of the *Avos* capture the essence of the Keil Sha-kai world that we live in. However, Hashem blessed us with tools to navigate the vicissitudes of life by also seeing the Name of Hashem that Moshe experienced. The Ramban in his commentary (*Shemos* 13:16) writes, "And from the great, revealed miracles, a person believes in the hidden miracles." It is specifically through the historical, clarifying experience of *geulas Mitzrayim* that Hashem directed Moshe to say to the Jewish people that He was also Hashem (*Shemos* 6:6). Even in our state of experiencing Hashem as Keil Sha-kai, sometimes it may feel that believing in Him is a challenge—in other words, not something that comes easily—and it is precisely the *geulas Mitzrayim* and similarly eye-opening "Hashem moments" in our lives that propel us to believe in His existence and all-encompassing involvement in the world.

In conclusion, the *pasuk* at the beginning of *Parashas Va'eira* is very relevant to our lives. *Galus* is such that it renders our relationship with Hashem as one of א-ל ש-ד-י and seeing Him as י-ק-ו-ק is challenging. However, we should learn from our *Avos*, who each developed their faith in Hashem under Keil Sha-kai circumstances, and be inspired by Hashem's eternal message to the Jewish people that He is also Hashem, as expressed in the Tetragrammaton.

· פרשת בא ·

PARASHAS BO

THE KORBAN PESACH: A MODEL FOR GEULAH

BY RABBI AARON LEIBTAG

As the Jewish people prepared to leave Egypt, we find there was only one challenge left for them: offering the *korban Pesach* (*Shemos*, ch. 12). Why was this the last step before they emerged as Am Yisrael? After almost a year had passed during which Hashem performed open miracles for them, we would expect that the Jewish people would now be ready to leave immediately. What was the purpose of the *korban Pesach*?

The answer is that the Jews needed to be actively involved in their own redemption. For most of the *geulah* process in Egypt, the Jewish people were spectators, seeing the powerful miracles that were part of the *makkos*. Yet they needed to become more engaged. In fact, in describing the mitzvah of *vehigadeta levincha*, the Rambam (*Hilchos Chametz U'matzah* 7:1) uses unique language:

אֲפִלּוּ חֲכָמִים גְּדוֹלִים חַיָּבִים לְסַפֵּר בִּיצִיאַת מִצְרַיִם וְכָל הַמַּאֲרִיךְ בִּדְבָרִים שֶׁאֵרְעוּ וְשֶׁהָיוּ הֲרֵי זֶה מְשֻׁבָּח.

Even great sages are required to recite the story of the Exodus from Egypt, and whoever extends this discussion of events *that occurred and that were* is praiseworthy.

Rabbi Yosef Dov Soloveitchik explains[9] that the Rambam employs both of these words, *she'eru*, that occurred, and *shehayu*, that were, to represent our process of redemption. *She'eru* describes the more passive role we had in Egypt. We didn't want to be in Egypt; we didn't want to be slaves. Yet we also took an active part in redemption: *shehayu*. We were participants, active and engaged. In the words of Rabbi Soloveitchik:

> In the processes of physical and enslavement and redemption the Jews were completely inactive. The Jew was not ready for *yetziat Mitzrayim*. He didn't expect the redemption to come immediately... This is *she-ir'u*—the events simply happened to them... However, spiritual redemption is different... Their acceptance of the Torah was part of a process of *gerut*, conversion, and involuntary *gerut* is impossible. The Jew, of his own free will, has chosen God. Since the Jew is an active participant in his spiritual redemption it is defined as *shehayu*.

As the final stage in the Jewish people's redemption, the *korban Pesach* provided them with the opportunity to grow. Four days before they left, Hashem indicated that until then, everything had been passive. Through the entire process of bringing the *korban Pesach*, the Jews were forced to extend beyond their comfort zones, thereby displaying a sign of faith and active participation in their redemption, moving from passive spectators to active participants.[10]

The great nineteenth-century German sage Rabbi Yaakov Tzvi

---

9. Rabbi Joseph B. Soloveitchik, *Festival of Freedom: Essays on Pesah and the Haggadah*, ed. Joel B. Wolowelsky and Reuven Ziegler (New York: Ktav Publishing House, 2006), 52–53.

10. Perhaps this is why the *korban Pesach* has been used throughout *Tanach* in the context of the Jewish people's renewal of their relationship with Hashem (see *Yehoshua* 5:10; *Melachim II* 23:21–22; *Divrei Hayamim II* 30:1, 29:10, 35:18; and Rabbi Kalisher's letter in 1836 to Mayer Amschel Rothschild encouraging him to purchase Har Habayis and/or gain the rights to bring *korbanos* there).

Mecklenburg, *zt"l*, notes in his work *Haketav Vehakabbalah* that "their fulfillment of every detail of this rite would be a proof of their complete faith in Hashem." As the lamb was the Egyptian god, this act of preparation and offering of the *korban* required an enormous level of *emunah* and *bitachon* in Hashem. Redemption of the Jewish people required them to both reaffirm their *emunah* in Him and at the same time become a part of the process.

When we reflect on *yetzias Mitzrayim* and its relevance to us today in retelling the story, we should remember that of all the miracles that occurred, perhaps the greatest one was the maturation of the Jewish people. They extended themselves, and in that struggle they succeeded in approaching Hashem in a more meaningful way. In our own lives, when we push ourselves to embrace the challenges and move beyond our comfort zones, it's there that we're able to uncover more of our potential and closeness to Hashem.[11]

---

11. For more on embracing the inconvenient and its ability to impact growth in our lives, see Tim Wu, "The Tyranny of Convenience," *New York Times*, February 16, 2018, https://www.nytimes.com/2018/02/16/opinion/sunday/tyranny-convenience. html, and Eytan Kobre, "The Easy Way Out," *Mishpacha*, March 14, 2018, http:// mishpacha.com/Browse/Article/9891/The-Easy-Way-Out.

· פרשת בשלח ·

PARASHAS BESHALACH

TAKING A LEAP OF FAITH

BY EFRAYIM PRERO

The Gemara in *Maseches Sotah* (37a) describes the scene leading up to *Kerias Yam Suf*. The tribes of Bnei Yisrael were standing at the edge of the Yam Suf, and each tribe declared they would not be going into the water first. Nachshon ben Aminadav jumped into the sea first, and then it split. Through this courageous act, Nachshon merited to be the first of the princes to bring his *korban* during the dedication of the Mishkan. The Midrash says (*Bamidbar Rabbah* 13:7) that Hashem said to Moshe, "The one who sanctified My Name in the water, he will bring his *korban* first."

Rabbi Chaim Shmuelevitz, *zt"l*, asks the following question in *Sichos Mussar* (*Parashas Mattos*): How is it possible that the tribes did not want to go into the Yam Suf first? Am Yisrael was built on *mesirus nefesh*, sacrificing one's life for the sake of Hashem. This is seen from the time Avraham offered Yitzchak as a *korban* at the *Akeidah*. Throughout the generations we have seen many instances of *mesirus nefesh*; how could it be that this generation was unable to "take the leap"?

Rabbi Chaim explains that had the command been to enter the Yam Suf and be done, surely all of the people would have jumped in. But when they saw the deep waters and the crashing waves, they couldn't envision this dangerous place to be the source of their salvation. Only Nachshon was on the level to be able to sanctify Hashem's Name. He understood full well the inherent dangers, but nonetheless disregarded them, as he was on a higher level of belief.

This understanding reflects the deeper meaning of the verse in *Yirmiyahu* (2:2):

כֹּה אָמַר ה' זָכַרְתִּי לָךְ חֶסֶד וגו' לֶכְתֵּךְ אַחֲרַי בַּמִּדְבָּר בְּאֶרֶץ לֹא זְרוּעָה.

So says Hashem: I remember the kindness of your youth…your following Me into the wilderness into an unsown land.

Bnei Yisrael is praised not in terms of the dangerous conditions of the desert, but rather because of their "following Me," following Hashem despite the physical circumstances.

Although Bnei Yisrael weren't on the level of Nachshon during *Kerias Yam Suf*, they did rise to his level during their travels in the desert. This can be seen from the gemara (*Shabbos* 31b) that says their travels were "*al pi Hashem*—through the words of Hashem." Every time they took down the Mishkan, it was without knowing what their next destination would be. They were simply following the word of Hashem.

A similar lesson can be learned from Chananiah, Mishael, and Azariah, who went into a fiery furnace and were saved. The Sages say (*Pesachim* 53b) they made a *kal vachomer* from the plague of the frogs in Egypt, which were likewise commanded to go into the ovens of the Egyptians and came out alive. They said to themselves, "If the frogs entered the ovens and were saved, we will be too." Rabbi Chaim Shmuelevitz asks: How is this *mesirus nefesh*? Knowing that they would be saved, it doesn't seem like they were risking anything. But according to the principle established, it makes perfect sense. The Sages are emphasizing not just that these men were *moser nefesh*, but that they disregarded the physical conditions and setting and instead totally trusted in Hashem, like Nachshon. They were willing not just to give up their lives, but even to totally disregard their surroundings.

In tough times we must continue to live in accordance with Hashem's will. He will deliver our salvation. *Mesirus nefesh* means depending on Hashem without knowing how we will make it through. By doing His will during the toughest times, we'll merit a salvation greater than the Exodus from Egypt and the splitting of the sea.

· פרשת יתרו ·

PARASHAS YISRO

1 BEFORE 1:
THE FIRST ANOCHI AT SINAI

BY RABBI MORDECAI TUROFF

The first of the *Aseres Hadibros* states, "*Anochi Hashem Eloke-cha*—I am Hashem your God" (*Shemos* 20:2).

The early commentators interpret this command in one of two ways: Either it is a command to believe in Hashem, or it is not a command at all, but the statement of a prerequisite for all mitzvos.[12] However, to better understand the *anochi* of the *Aseres Hadibros*, we will focus on another fundamental idea expressed in this parashah, one that hearkens to an even earlier *anochi* taught at Sinai.

Parashas Yisro begins by reintroducing us to Moshe Rabbeinu's family. We meet his father-in-law, Yisro; Moshe's wife, Tzipporah; and their two sons, Gershom and Eliezer. The Torah tells us that Moshe's eldest was named Gershom, "*Ki amar ger hayisi be'eretz nochriyah*—For he said: 'I have been a stranger in a strange land'" (ibid. 18:3). While it is not unusual for the Torah to tell us the meaning and reason behind a name, in the case of Gershom it is indeed remarkable, for the Torah, sixteen chapters earlier, in *Parashas Shemos*, introduced us to Gershom and gave us the meaning and reason behind his name: "*Vateiled ben vayikra es shemo Gershom ki amar ger hayisi be'eretz nochriyah*—And she bore a son, and he called his name Gershom; for he said: 'I have been a stranger in a strange land'" (ibid. 2:22). The *pasuk*

---

12. See Rambam and Ramban, *Sefer Hamitzvos*, asei 1. See also Rabbi Samson Raphael Hirsch, *Collected Writings of Rabbi Samson Raphael Hirsch*, vol. 2 (New York: Feldheim, 1996), 138–43.

in *Parashas Yisro* is a carbon copy of the *pasuk* in *Parashas Shemos*! What is the Torah trying to teach us by repeating verbatim the meaning behind this name?

The name Gershom calls to mind a great-uncle of Moshe Rabbeinu's who had a very similar name. Levi, Moshe's great-grandfather, had three sons, and the eldest was Gershon. The Shelah Hakadosh (*Parashas Va'eira, Derech Chaim, Tochachas Mussar*) writes:

הָעִנְיָן הוּא, כִּי שֵׁבֶט לֵוִי לֹא הָיוּ בַּגָּלוּת, וְלֵוִי יָדַע דָּבָר זֶה, וְרָצָה לְהִשְׁתַּתֵּף בְּצָרַת הַצִּבּוּר. מֶה עָשָׂה, קָרָא שֵׁמוֹת לְבָנָיו עַל שֵׁם הַגָּלוּת, דְּהַיְנוּ שֵׁם 'גֵּרְשׁוֹן' עַל שֵׁם 'כִּי גֵרִים הֵם בְּאֶרֶץ לֹא לָהֶם'.

> The idea was that since the tribe of Levi was not in exile [they weren't enslaved], and Levi himself knew this was going to be the case, he named his sons after the exile, which is why his son Gershon was named [according to the verse] "they will be sojourners in a land that isn't theirs."

In other words, because Levi was not subjected to the slavery in Egypt, he gave his children names to elicit feelings of empathy. The name Gershon, similar to Gershom, conveys a message: Despite one's level of comfort—whether one is among the Levi'im living in freedom in Egypt or in Moshe Rabbeinu's family living in the lap of luxury in Midian—one must connect to the suffering of the community. Gershon/Gershom means we can never be complacent as long as another Jew is in pain.

This notion of being *mishtatef betzaras hatzibbur*, of participating in public suffering, is a tradition that may have been passed down in Moshe's family, but it was also a lesson Moshe learned from Hashem Himself at Sinai, even before ascending the mountain to receive the Torah.

In *Parashas Shemos* (3:2), Hashem spoke to Moshe at the *har haElokim*, the mountain of Hashem, from the burning bush, which was in the same geographic location as Har Sinai. The *Midrash Tanchuma*

(*Parashas Shemos* 14) asks about this first time Hashem spoke to Moshe from the bush:

לָמָה מִתּוֹךְ הַסְּנֶה וְלֹא מִתּוֹךְ אִילָן אַחֵר, אָמַר הַקָּבָּ"ה 'עִמּוֹ אָנֹכִי בְצָרָה'.

Why from a thorny bush and not another tree? Hashem said "With him I will participate in the suffering."

The thorny bush represents Hashem's presence even amid suffering. Hashem's introductory lesson at Sinai, the first time He used the word *anochi*, I, was this lesson about participation in public suffering. This highlights that *Matan Torah* and its axiomatic belief in Hashem is predicated on a system of sensitivity toward others.

It is no coincidence that the idea of *imo Anochi vetzarah* was taught at Har Sinai, the future site of *Matan Torah*. The Mishnah in *Avos* (6:6) tells us that one of the forty-eight values needed to acquire the Torah is to be *nosei be'ol chaveiro*, to carry (share) a friend's burden. In other words, before we can internalize the first commandment of *Anochi Hashem*, we have to learn to accept the *anochi* of *imo Anochi vetzarah*, of participating in the suffering of friends and community.

Along the same lines, we can suggest that the Torah repeats the meaning of Gershom's name at the beginning of the parashah of *Matan Torah* to emphasize the value of *nosei be'ol chaveiro*. Before Moshe Rabbeinu ascended the mountain on behalf of the Jewish people, the Torah shines light on the fact that he was worthy of such a task because he truly was *mishtatef betzaras hatzibbur*. Even when not in close physical proximity to a suffering Jew, he was always connected, "*Ki amar ger hayisi be'eretz nochriyah*—For he said, 'I am a stranger in a strange land.'"

Perhaps *imo Anochi vetzarah*, the idea of being *nosei be'ol chaveiro*, is a prerequisite to accepting the Torah because the very belief in *Anochi Hashem*, the basis for belief in and adherence to the rest of the Torah, requires this appreciation. Rabbi Samson Raphael Hirsch, in his commentary on the *Chumash* (*Shemos* 20:2), states: "אנכי...reveals the speaker as a personality who is intimately close to the one addressed, a personality who encompasses bears and supports the one addressed."

The two instances of *anochi* tell us that we not only believe in a God, but we believe in a God Who is present in our lives at all times. In order to accept the Torah and appreciate the beliefs therein, we must be able to connect and empathize with those in need. We must strive to model this first *anochi* that came before the more famous *anochi*. In doing so, we will merit being worthy of the "*retzon shochni sneh*—the goodwill of the One Who dwells in the bush" (*Devarim* 33:16),13 the blessing of a God Who teaches *imo Anochi vetzarah*.

---

13. See Maharal, *Gur Aryeh* (*Devarim* 33:16), who writes: "Since Hashem revealed Himself originally in the bush [in accordance with the *pasuk*] 'imo Anochi vetzarah' (*Tehillim* 91:15), this the greatest goodwill."

· פרשת משפטים ·

PARASHAS MISHPATIM

YOU DO YOUR PIECE

BY RABBI EZRA SHAPIRO

The transition from *Parashas Yisro* to *Parashas Mishpatim* is jarring and confusing. The Jewish people experienced *Matan Torah*. We were designated as *am hanivchar,* the chosen people. The Midrash states that we were distinguished from other nations by our willingness to commit to the Torah before hearing what was in it, as expressed via the famous phrase "*Na'aseh venishma*—We will do, and [then] we will hear" (*Shemos* 24:7). The Kuzari asserts that this event is the source of our national spiritual identity.

From there we shift immediately to *Parashas Mishpatim*, which is centered around how to react not only *if* we go awry but *when* we go awry. There is guidance regarding how to proceed when a Jew plans to kill a fellow Jew, and when a Jew damages a fellow Jew. What a harsh splash of cold water! The metaphor conjured up is of a boy receiving an acceptance letter into an illustrious yeshivah. The letter colorfully but honestly delineates the opportunities which lie ahead in his joining unique cadre of *talmidim* striving to become genuine *talmidei chachamim.* The second page of the letter includes guidelines for an incoming *talmid.* It outlines whom he should turn to when his roommate steals his money, what he should do the first time his friends speak behind his back and destroy his reputation. But why now? What kind of elite group of students is he actually joining?

To properly appreciate this transition requires an understanding of the relationship between goals and responsibility in *avodas Hashem.* The premise of our confusion is that there is a goal which is holy, and that success and holiness is measured by achieving that goal. In that case, indeed, *Parashas Mishpatim* provides a jarring dose of reality, a picture of an unholy nation. However, in the writings of the Ramchal and Rabbi Dessler (*Michtav MeEliyahu*) we see a different model. In it, our goals are not the measure of success; the goals act as the compass which guides and directs our choices, responsibilities, and efforts. And it is the choices and efforts themselves which are the determinants of our success and *sechar*. *They* should be the source of gratification, not the attainment of the goal. *Parashas Yisro* presents a compass of holiness; only after that are we presented with the challenges we will encounter along the path to holiness.

The prophet Yeshaya rebukes King Chizkiyahu for refraining from marrying and having children because of a prophetic dream King Chizkiyahu had that his child would be a wicked king. Yeshaya's rebuke expresses our very point (*Berachos* 10a):

בַּהֲדֵי כְּבְשֵׁי דְּרַחֲמָנָא לָמָה לָךְ, מַאי דְּמִפַּקְדַתְּ אִבָּעֵי לָךְ לְמֶעֱבַד, וּמַה דְּנִיחָא קַמֵּהּ קֻדְשָׁא בְּרִיךְ הוּא לָעֲבִיד.

To paraphrase, Yeshaya says to King Chizkiyahu that the result is not his responsibility; his concern is to follow the Torah. What Hashem does with that effort is His responsibility. We are often understandably frustrated when our *mesirus nefesh*, the efforts we make, in *chinuch banim*, in health, or in *shidduchim* do not necessarily generate the noble results we dream of. It's so important to remind ourselves that our success, and in turn our satisfaction, is contingent only on our responsibility and effort, not on the way Hashem decides to pave the path which lies before us. The rules in *Parashas Mishpatim* actually represent part of our path to holiness and not at all the fall from grace that they seem to be describing at first glance.

· פרשת תרומה ·

PARASHAS TERUMAH

THE OHR ḤACHAIM ON
WHAT IS TRULY VALUABLE

BY RABBI SHMUEL L. SCHUMAN

At the beginning of *Parashas Terumah* the Torah lists the various materials the Jewish people donated for the construction of the Mishkan. The list begins with precious metals in order of their value—gold, silver, copper—followed by various less valuable items such as textiles, leather, wood, oil, and spices. Oddly, the most valuable items of all—the precious stones used for the *ephod* and *choshen* worn by the *kohen gadol*—are placed at the end of the list. It would seem more appropriate for the Torah to put the more expensive, precious gems at the very beginning of the list, before the gold and silver. What is the purpose of this seeming inconsistency in the listing of the donated materials?

The Ohr Hachaim offers three answers, each with an important lesson for us about giving.

The first answer he gives is that the *nesi'im*, the princes of each tribe, donated these precious stones to the Mishkan. However, they donated them last, only after they saw that the Jewish people had brought everything else needed for the Mishkan. The Midrash (*Bamidbar Rabbah* 12:16, brought by Rashi to *Shemos* 35:27) says that Hashem was displeased with this lack of alacrity on the part of the *nesi'im*. As a result, He symbolically removed the letter *yud* from their title later on in *Parashas Vayakhel* (*Shemos* 35:27), where the Torah records that the *nesi'im* donated these precious stones. For this reason, in our parashah Hashem placed the precious stones last on the list to indicate that to Hashem they are inferior to all the other items even though they are the most materially precious.

The Ohr Hachaim stresses earlier (ibid. 25:2) that all donations were to come from the heart. Not giving immediately and in a timely manner demonstrates a lack of enthusiasm in the donor and is thus substandard.

Rabbi Meir Segal shared a powerful memory of Rabbi Chaim Shmuelevitz that he personally witnessed. Rabbi Segal was in attendance at an engagement party in 1971 of a fellow Mirrer Yeshivah *talmid*, when unexpectedly Rabbi Chaim Shmuelevitz appeared. Rabbi Chaim spoke to the gathering about this very *pasuk* and the Ohr Hachaim's comment above. He then turned to the *chasan* and said, "*Yungerman*, you are about to get married. Realize if you buy your *kallah* the most valuable birthday or anniversary gift but give it to her late, it won't be worth much." True giving from the heart is manifest only when giving promptly and enthusiastically.

The second answer the Ohr Hachaim gives is this. The Gemara (*Yoma* 69a) says that the *kohanim* were permitted to derive personal benefit from the priestly garments even though it was generally forbidden (under the prohibition known as *me'ilah*) to do so with other items that belonged to the Mishkan. In this sense, the priestly garments were not as holy as the other articles used for furnishing the Mishkan or for performing its service.

Accordingly, the precious stones are listed last because all other donated materials were used for the needs of the Mishkan itself or its service, as opposed to the precious stones, which were used only for the priestly garments—for the *ephod* and the *choshen*. Since it was permitted to derive benefit from the garments into which these precious stones were placed, their degree of holiness was less than that of the other materials donated to the Mishkan, and therefore they are listed last.

We see that an item with little material value used exclusively for holy purposes is more valuable than an item of great material value used for one's personal benefit, even if also used for holy purposes. So too, giving less with no personal gain is more valuable in Hashem's eyes than giving more while personally benefiting. To the extent that we gain something out of giving, that gain lessens the holiness of our giving.

A similar idea can be learned from an explanation of Rabbi Yochanan Zweig, *shlita*, on a well-known mishnah in *Pirkei Avos*. One of the pillars on which the world stands is *gemilus chasadim,* granting acts of kindness (*Avos* 1:2). What is the significance of the word *gemilus*, granting? Why not just say that *chasadim* is one of the pillars on which the world stands? Rabbi Zweig explains this based on the *pasuk* in *Bereishis* (21:8):

וַיִּגְדַּל הַיֶּלֶד וַיִּגָּמַל וַיַּעַשׂ אַבְרָהָם מִשְׁתֶּה גָדוֹל בְּיוֹם הִגָּמֵל אֶת יִצְחָק.

The child grew up and was weaned, and Avraham held a great feast on the day that Yitzchak was weaned.

The word *gamal* means "wean." The intent of the phrase *gemilus chasadim* is that *chesed* should be done altruistically, weaning oneself out of the act of *chesed* by not deriving personal benefit or honor from it. The more one weans oneself from the *chesed*, the greater the *chesed* performed.

The third answer the Ohr Hachaim provides is as follows. Another gemara (*Yoma* 75a) says that the clouds brought the precious stones to the desert to make them available for the people to donate them to the Mishkan. Meaning, the stones that the people donated had been delivered to them by Hashem, without their having invested any effort in acquiring them and without any out-of-pocket expense. Thus, the Torah lists the precious stones after all the materials that the people bought from their own pockets, and that they acquired with effort in order to donate, because a donation involving personal expense and effort is more precious to Hashem than a donation that involves no personal expense or effort.

This teaches us that an item given as a gift is much more meaningful if one gave up something to obtain it. When a person has "skin in the game" to acquire an object or money or to achieve a goal, it truly belongs to him. So when he then gives up that object or achievement for another person, it's very meaningful because he gave up something that he truly owned.

We live in a very material world. While that's a blessing we must truly appreciate, it also presents a challenge for us to accurately identify and prioritize what is really valuable. The placement of the precious stones at the end of the list of materials donated to the Mishkan helps us understand that Hashem's value system emphasizes that what matters most is not the material value of things. The Ohr Hachaim demonstrates that what is genuinely valuable depends on how and when something is given, how pure and holy is its use, and how much "skin in the game" one invested to get it.

When we show effort, we're demonstrating to Hashem our yearning for a relationship. Through dedicating ourselves to *kedushah* and making costly choices instead of the most convenient ones, we reveal that our relationship with Hashem is more precious than exquisite gems.

· פרשת תצוה ·

PARASHAS TETZAVEH

THE ULTIMATE PURPOSE
OF THE MISHKAN

BY RABBI YOSSI GOLDIN

P*arashas Tetzaveh* begins in the middle of the discussion regarding the commandments to construct the Mishkan and its accompanying structures, vessels, and garments. In the previous parashah, *Parashas Terumah*, the Torah describes the Mishkan's structure and vessels, and this parashah continues that theme by describing the elegant clothing that the *kohen gadol* wore during his service in the Mishkan. It then transitions to the process of anointing the Mishkan and the vessels that would be used within it. The Torah then outlines the *korban tamid*, the continuous offering, which was brought every morning and evening, and ends with a description of how to construct the *mizbei'ach haketores*, the incense altar.

If we look closely at the pattern above, one aspect seems to be out of place, namely, the description of the *korban tamid*. As we mentioned, the rest of these two parshiyos deal with the description of constructing the Mishkan, its vessels and garments, and the process of consecration. In general, all descriptions of the sacrifices themselves are saved for *Parashas Vayikra*, where they are outlined in great detail. So why does the Torah digress here to make mention of the contents of the *korban tamid*?

Rabbi Samson Raphael Hirsch, in his commentary on the Torah, gives a beautiful explanation for the seeming digression. He explains (*Shemos* 29:38) as follows:

… it is not the establishment and consecration of the Sanctuary and priests that by itself brings about the promised goal of Hashem's presence in the nation… It is only achieved when the Sanctuary becomes alive and active through the acts of devotion of the people which is to be equivalent to the heartbeat, the central driving force of the national life.[14]

In order to stress that the ultimate purpose and goal of the creation of the Mishkan was the *avodah* and constant service that would take place within it on a daily basis, the Torah makes sure to include a description of the daily *korban tamid* within a description of the construction and consecration of the Mishkan.

Nowadays, we don't have the Mishkan or the Beis Hamikdash, and our shuls and homes act as a type of sanctuary within which we do our best to serve Hashem. Our parashah reminds us that while these outer buildings are important and should reflect the sanctity that is created within, ultimately it is not the outer structures themselves that determine the *kedushah*, but the daily service, the day-to-day encounters with Hashem, His Torah, and His mitzvos that we cultivate within these buildings that are important.

Many commentators point out the same thing regarding the *tefillah* that takes places within our shuls and homes. While the content of *tefillah* and the way it is said is certainly important and should be done correctly, what is most important is the *kavanah*, the intention behind the *tefillah*, and the connection and spirituality that it creates. If we say the correct words, but by rote and without thought, there is a limit to the effect that those *tefillos* can have. However, if our *tefillos* become the vehicle through which we cultivate a relationship with Hashem and strengthen our belief in Him and His Torah, then our *tefillos* will truly have an effect on us and our Judaism.

---

14. Rabbi Samson Raphael Hirsch, *The Pentateuch* (New York: Judaica Press, 1971).

· פרשת כי תשא ·

PARASHAS KI SISA

ALL FOR THE BOSS: SERVING HASHEM WHEN WE DON'T UNDERSTAND

BY RABBI AVI FRIED

Parashas Ki Sisa discusses the tragedy of the *eigel hazahav*, the golden calf. This particularly dark moment in the Jewish people's history occurred when the Jews danced around a golden idol that they had fashioned while waiting for Moshe to receive the *aseres hadibros* from Hashem.

The *chet ha'eigel* presents a daunting question: Having just heard Hashem's voice at Har Sinai, how could the Jewish people have betrayed Him so quickly? Various commentators explain that in fashioning the idol, the Jews were not trying to create a new god, but rather attempting to replace Moshe with a new leader (see *Da'as Zekeinim* and *Ba'alei HaTosafos* on *Shemos* 32:1).

The Netziv explains that the Jewish nation thought that only through Moshe did they receive their sustenance from Above and that he enabled them to survive in this special spiritual state. When Moshe had not yet returned from Sinai, the Jews panicked, thinking that they would be unable to survive their desert travails without him.

Yet even with the Netziv's explanation in mind, loss of one's leader does not justify betrayal of Hashem. Why did the Jews, who had just witnessed miracles no one before them had ever seen, dance around an idol?

Perhaps the incident of the *eigel hazahav* must be viewed in context to better understand the dilemma the Jewish nation faced. The Jewish people had just stood at Sinai—an event unparalleled in history—as well as seen Hashem's outstretched hand guiding them forth from Egypt. Once accustomed to this high level of spirituality, they could not comprehend departing from it. By building the golden idol, they were not lowering themselves. As the Maharal (*Gur Aryeh, Shemos* 32:1) explains, if anything, the Jews merely were trying to maintain their lofty spiritual state:

וְלָמָּה הָיוּ רוֹצִים לַעֲשׂוֹת אֱלֹהִים בִּמְקוֹמוֹ שֶׁל מֹשֶׁה, אֶלָּא פֵּרוּשׁוֹ שֶׁ'יִהְיֶה מוֹרֶה לָנוּ הַדֶּרֶךְ', וְעַכְשָׁו אָנוּ צְרִיכִין לֵאלָהוּת. וּמִפְּנֵי שֶׁיָּדְעוּ בְּמַדְרֵגָתוֹ שֶׁל מֹשֶׁה וּבְמַעֲלָתוֹ, וְיָדְעוּ אֲשֶׁר אֵין אֱלֹהִים אֲשֶׁר יַעֲשׂוּ יִהְיֶה בְּמַדְרֵגָתוֹ, הָיוּ מִתְאַוִּים לֵאלָהוּת הַרְבֵּה, וְהָיוּ רוֹצִים לְהַגִּיעַ אֶל מַדְרֵיגַת מֹשֶׁה בֵּאֱלֹהוּת הַרְבֵּה שֶׁיִּהְיֶה לָהֶם.

Why did they want to make a god in place of Moshe? The explanation of the matter is that [originally] they wanted "a leader," [but] now they need a god. Because they knew of the level of Moshe and his greatness, and they knew that Hashem wouldn't create another on his level, they desired a lot of godliness. They wanted to reach the level of Moshe in his godliness.

According to this explanation, the Jewish people's conduct was indeed well intended, but the *eigel hazahav* demonstrated that their relationship with Hashem was one-sided. They expected to be served, when in fact they should have been serving Hashem.

Had they only cared about serving Hashem, they would not have panicked when Moshe did not appear immediately. Instead, they quickly lost faith and calculated on their own what they needed to do to maintain their spirituality. They should have realized that the same God Who had performed miracles on their behalf until that time would continue to protect them in the desert. The Jews desired immediate assurance when they would have been better served to trust in eventual Divine intervention. Not surprisingly, Moshe asked those Jews who still believed in Hashem to help him quell the chaos that ensued with the creation of the *eigel hazahav*.

The Jewish people seemingly did not know how to incorporate the pristine spiritual level they garnered at Sinai into their everyday lives. Accustomed to the supernatural awe of Hashem, they didn't realize that true belief dictates that adherents serve Hashem even when they don't feel this exalted spiritual state. Even when Moshe did not descend Sinai quickly, the Jews should have exhibited a greater belief in the Divine ability to solve their problems. They needed to understand that Jews must serve Hashem not only when life is going well, but even when clarity is lacking and the situation seems hopeless.

In contrast to the general populace, the Levi'im truly believed in Hashem, killing their brothers who had worshipped the *eigel hazahav*. Performing the difficult task of slaying fellow members of their nation, the Levi'im put aside their personal misgivings and fulfilled Hashem's words admirably.

The *chet ha'eigel* had various consequences. For example, as a result of the Jewish people's lack of faith, Hashem no longer directly led them in the desert. For this same reason, Hashem removed the special crowns that He had fashioned for them at Sinai. The Jews had earned their crowns by stating that they would first accept the Torah and then later hear about its precepts (*na'aseh venishma*). Their conduct at the time of the *eigel hazahav* was diametrically opposed to their prior behavior when accepting the Torah. Rather than maintaining their belief during a time of doubt, the Jewish people panicked. They built an idol out of fear and therefore lost the crowns that they had previously earned through their blind trust in Hashem.

Aside from the metaphysical removal of the Jewish nation's crowns, the *chet ha'eigel* had some important physical ramifications. For example, whereas Hashem fashioned the first set of *luchos* with His own finger (*Shemos* 31:18), Moshe made the second set of *luchos*, and Hashem merely inscribed them. Additionally, the Ramban posits that in contrast to the first Sinai meeting, during the second giving of the *luchos*, the Jews were unable to physically approach the mountain. And finally, following the giving of the second *luchos*, Hashem's presence began to dwell far outside the camp.

The verse says, "And Moshe took the tent and planted it outside the camp, far from the camp, and he called it the Tent of Meeting. All who sought Hashem had to travel to the Tent of Meeting that lay outside the camp" (ibid. 33:7). Interestingly, the beginning of the verse states that Moshe planted the Mishkan outside the camp, whereas the end of the verse says that Jews seeking Hashem now had to travel outside the camp to seek Him. Seemingly, the verse labels Moshe as Hashem. Rabbeinu Bachya explains that because Moshe had connected himself to Hashem, the Torah called him by Hashem's Name, in the same way that a messenger is often referred to by the name of the person who appointed or sent him.

Perhaps we can also explain that the Jewish nation misplaced their trust. They trusted Moshe instead of Hashem, and when Moshe didn't return, they lost faith in him as well. The Jews thought that without Moshe they could not continue, but if they had served Hashem whole-heartedly, they would have realized that life in the desert would go on as normal. The verse stresses that the Jews now needed to trust in Hashem. Even though Moshe had replanted the tent, the Torah characterizes the searching Jews as those "who sought Hashem," not Moshe. The Torah wanted to stress that the Jews should never have been seeking Moshe in the first place. To Hashem they owed their existence, and upon Him they should have depended.

Later in the parashah (ibid. 32:34), Rashi posits that the sin of the *eigel hazahav* lives forever, and its footprints can be seen in the future tragedies that befell the Jewish people:

וְאֵין פּוּרְעָנוּת בָּאָה עַל יִשְׂרָאֵל שָׁאֵין בָּהּ קְצָת מִפִּרְעוֹן עֲוֹן הָעֵגֶל.

Evils do not come on the Israelites that do not have some [remnant] of the sin of the [golden] calf.

What does Rashi mean by this cryptic phrase? Perhaps he intends to hint at the base trait the Jewish people exhibited when dancing around the *eigel hazahav*. As discussed above, it showed that the Jews had a lack of faith, an inability to conform to the lofty ideal of *na'aseh venishma* that they had previously professed to believe. When tragedies happen to the Jewish people, invariably the Jews will have shouldered some of the blame—whether it be a lack of faith on their part or an inability to truly subjugate themselves to their Master.

According to Rashi, to avoid future tragedies, Jews must first realize that service to Hashem is not based on one's personal motivations. Even when one doesn't fully understand a predicament or feel that Hashem cares, one must still serve Him and believe in His salvation. Jews cannot trust in individuals to whom they attribute extreme spiritual powers. Each Jew must connect to Hashem individually and not rely on a Moshe-like figure to connect to Him for them.

It remains the task of all of us to recall the mistake of our ancestors as they danced around the *eigel hazahav* and reaffirm to ourselves our duty and willingness to trust in Hashem with love. While idol worship itself today does not dominate society as it did back then, the threat of improper influences does. All of us are surrounded by an endless number of negative forces that pull us away from Hashem. We sometimes do not feel spiritually connected or comprehend a situation, but nevertheless, we must maintain our faith. May we all be blessed with maintaining belief and service of Hashem in the face of diminished motivation and understanding.

· פרשת ויקהל ·

PARASHAS VAYAKHEL

SHABBOS AND CHOL:
LIVING WITH CONSISTENCY

BY RABBI YONI FOX

P*arashas Vayakhel* begins with one of the many references to the mitzvah of Shabbos that appear throughout the Torah (*Shemos* 35:2):

שֵׁשֶׁת יָמִים תֵּעָשֶׂה מְלָאכָה וּבַיּוֹם הַשְּׁבִיעִי יִהְיֶה לָכֶם קֹדֶשׁ שַׁבַּת שַׁבָּתוֹן לַה' כָּל הָעֹשֶׂה בוֹ מְלָאכָה יוּמָת.

Six days do work and on the seventh it shall be for you a Sabbath for Hashem; whomever does work shall perish.

As in other contexts, the Torah introduces the mitzvah to refrain from work on Shabbos by referring to the permissibility of *melachah* throughout the week.[15] What is the relevance of one's weekday activities to the holiness of Shabbos?

By consistently linking these two concepts, the Torah seems to indicate that there is in fact a fundamental connection between the performance of work during the week and the prohibition against doing *melachah* on Shabbos. The nature of this relationship is described differently by various commentators. The author of the *Turei Zahav* explains that the Shabbos experience is enhanced by one's conduct during

---

15. See *Mechilta, Parashah Alef,* as to the distinction between the language of *te'aseh* that appears here and *ta'aseh* that appears in *Parashas Mishpatim*.

the week. In order to be able to properly experience the *kedushah* of Shabbos, one must spiritually prepare oneself during the six weekdays. On the other hand, Rabbi Tzadok Hakohen of Lublin, *zt"l*, in his *sefer Pri Tzaddik* (*Parashas Emor*), states that Shabbos has the ability to elevate one's weekday activities; by dedicating one's actions throughout the week to preparing for Shabbos, one infuses the *kedushah* of Shabbos into all that he does. Alternatively, the Ohr Hachaim says that proper observance of Shabbos enhances one's weekday experience in a different manner. If one treats Shabbos with the proper *kedushah*, the remaining six days will suffice for him to address his material needs.

Rabbi Shlomo Breuer, *zt"l*, in his work *Chochmah U'mussar*, presents a different approach. He explains that Shabbos represents our *emunah* in Hashem as the Creator of the world. Engaging in *melachah*, creative activity, expresses man's mastery over creation; the cessation from *melachah* on Shabbos demonstrates the recognition that man is not truly master of the world. However, in order for Shabbos to serve as a meaningful expression of this idea, it must be reflected in one's weekday activities as well. If the *emunah* one conveys through his Shabbos observance is sincere, it must guide his conduct throughout the other six days. Only by living life with a consistency that is reflected in both the *melachah* in which one engages during the week as well as in refraining from *melachah* on Shabbos does one truly express the *emunah* that Shabbos is supposed to convey.

The idea of *emunah* demanding consistency in one's life is expressed in the writings of Rabbi Breuer's father-in-law, Rabbi Samson Raphael Hirsch, as well. Rabbi Hirsch explains that the *pasuk* of Shema that says, "*Shema Yisrael Hashem Elokeinu Hashem Echad*" conveys a belief in Hashem as the sole power that controls the world. The next *pasuk*, "*Ve'ahavta es Hashem Elokecha bechol levavecha u'vechol nafshecha u'vechol me'odecha*," seems to be a profession of love for Hashem. What is the connection? How does love flow from a recognition of Hashem's Oneness? Rabbi Hirsch explains that the focus is in the word *bechol*, with all; the recognition that Hashem is the one true power demands a complete devotion to Him. Genuine *emunah*, expressed by the words *Shema Yisrael*, evokes a dedication to Hashem that pervades every aspect of one's life. Recognition of the unity of Hashem unifies our own lives as well.

When one truly internalizes *emunah*, it creates a reality of *shivisi Hashem lenegdi samid* (*Shulchan Aruch, Orach Chaim* 1:1), that Hashem is a constant presence in one's life. One lives every aspect of his life, both the days of Shabbos and the seemingly mundane days of the week, with consistency, rather than living a compartmentalized life. Perhaps this is the intent of our Sages when they say (*Makkos* 24a):

בָּא חֲבַקּוּק וְהֶעֱמִידָן עַל אַחַת, שֶׁנֶּאֱמַר 'וְצַדִּיק בֶּאֱמוּנָתוֹ יִחְיֶה'.

Chavakuk said that the whole Torah is dependent upon one fundamental value: that a tzaddik should live with *emunah*.

Emunah is the most basic principle that guides and unifies everything we do.

PARASHAS PEKUDEI

TWO MODELS OF THE MISHKAN

BY DR. ELIE PORTNOY

Parashas Pekudei marks the completion of *Sefer Shemos* and the process of *hakamas haMishkan*, erecting the Tabernacle, which began several parshiyos earlier. There are at least two diverging opinions among the commentators about the role and centrality of the Mishkan in the Jewish people's life in the desert. On the one extreme is the opinion of the Ramban. According to the Ramban, the Mishkan was always intended to be a central part of Klal Yisrael's communal life in the desert. Its role was to serve as a continuation of the experience of *gilui Shechinah*, Divine revelation, which occurred at Sinai. This is best expressed in his commentary at the beginning of *Parashas Terumah* (*Shemos* 25:2):

'וְאַתֶּם תִּהְיוּ לִי מַמְלֶכֶת כֹּהֲנִים וְגוֹי קָדוֹשׁ', וְהִנֵּה הֵם קְדוֹשִׁים, רְאוּיִים שֶׁיִּהְיֶה בָּהֶם מִקְדָּשׁ לְהַשְׁרוֹת שְׁכִינָתוֹ בֵּינֵיהֶם. וּלְכָךְ צִוָּה תְּחִלָּה עַל דְּבַר הַמִּשְׁכָּן, שֶׁיִּהְיֶה לוֹ בַּיִת בְּתוֹכָם מְקֻדָּשׁ לִשְׁמוֹ... וְסוֹד הַמִּשְׁכָּן הוּא שֶׁיִּהְיֶה הַכָּבוֹד אֲשֶׁר שָׁכַן עַל הַר סִינַי.

"You shall be to Me a kingdom of priests and a holy nation..." It was befitting that they should have a Temple for the Shechinah to dwell among them, and that is why they were commanded to build the Mishkan, as a continuation of the experience of Sinai. The secret of the Mishkan is that it should have the glory that Hashem [bestowed] at Har Sinai.

The Ramban's opinion that the Mishkan had always been intended to play a role for the Jewish people goes hand in hand with his general approach to the order of the parshiyos, which is that *yeish mukdam u'me'uchar baTorah*, that the order in which the events are presented does generally represent their original chronological order. In all circumstances, where possible, we try to explain the order as being chronologically sequenced. The fact that the commandment to build the Mishkan was given before the sin that occurred later in *Parashas Ki Sisa* indicates that in no way did it serve as an atonement for that later mistake. This opinion is shared by others, including Ibn Ezra.

In contrast to the Ramban's opinion lies the alternative extreme, the opinion of the Sforno, among others. The Sforno alludes to this in *Shemos* (31:18):

מִפְּנֵי מָה לֹא הָשַּׂג הַתַּכְלִית שֶׁיָּעַד הָקֵ-ל יִתְבָּרַךְ בְּמַתַּן הַתּוֹרָה בְּאָמְרוֹ 'וְאַתֶּם תִּהְיוּ לִי מַמְלֶכֶת כֹּהֲנִים וְגוֹי קָדוֹשׁ' ... עַד שֶׁהָצְרַךְ לַעֲשׂוֹת מִשְׁכָּן ... וְהוֹדִיעַ שֶׁקָּרָה זֶה בְּסִבַּת רֹעַ בְּחִירַת יִשְׂרָאֵל ... וְהֵמָּה מָרוּ וְהִשְׁחִיתוּ דַּרְכָּם וְנָפְלוּ מִמַּעֲלָתָם.

What is the reason that [the Jews] never attained the goal of the giving of the Torah of Hashem's designation that "you shall be to Me a kingdom of priests and a holy nation"... [so much so that it] even required us to build a Mishkan...? This is because of the evil choice of Bnei Yisrael...that they rebelled and were destructive and fell from their high stature.

According to the Sforno, until Klal Yisrael committed the *chet ha'eigel* they were simply not "*hutzrach la'asos Mishkan*—in need of a Mishkan"; only because of the "*sibas ro'a bechiras Yisrael*—the evil choosing of the Jewish people" did the less ideal situation arise, which would necessitate the construction of a Mishkan (see also the Sforno on *Shemos* 25:9 and *Vayikra* 11:2, which states that the Mishkan is a product of the *chet ha'eigel*).

In truth, the opinions of both the Sforno and the Ramban above are clearly reflected in various differing midrashim, reflecting parallel diverging opinions among our Sages about the Mishkan's specific role in the desert (see *Midrash Tanchuma*, *Parashas Terumah* 8, and *Yerushalmi Shekalim* 2b versus *Bamidbar Rabbah* 13).

An apparently third opinion is put forward by Rashi. At first glance, at the beginning of *Parashas Pekudei*, Rashi makes a statement, seemingly in line with the Sforno. The new Mishkan is called the *Mishkan Ha'eidus*, the Tabernacle of Testimony. Rashi comments (*Shemos* 38:21):

עֵדוּת לְיִשְׂרָאֵל שֶׁוִּתֵּר לָהֶם הַקָּבָּ"ה עַל מַעֲשֵׂה הָעֵגֶל, שֶׁהֲשְׁרָה שְׁכִינָתוֹ
בֵּינֵיהֶם.

Testimony to Israel, to the fact that Hashem forgave them for the *eigel hazahav* incident and the Shechinah dwells among them.

Rashi makes an even more overt comment in *Shemos* 31:18. In both cases, he seems to indicate that the Mishkan would serve as an atonement for the *eigel hazahav*, seemingly a *bedieved* scenario, and also rooted in his frequently cited opinion that *ein mukdam u'me'uchar baTorah*, that the Torah is not written in chronological sequence. The Mishkan may come first in the Torah, but this does not reflect what occurred chronologically. (For further elucidation on the need for the reversed order in the Torah, see Rabbeinu Bachya's opinion [*Shemos* 25:6] of *makdim refuah lemakkah*.)

However, twice Rashi (*Shemos* 25:5, 26:15) seems to indicate an idea to the contrary. His opinion is that the Mishkan was actually an anticipated event, conceived well before the *chet ha'eigel*. Many question how Bnei Yisrael acquired the *atzei shittim* used to build the Mishkan in the desert. Rashi (ibid.) cites a midrash that when Yaakov went to Egypt to reunite with Yosef, he saw through prophecy that Bnei Yisrael would one day build a Mishkan in the desert. Yaakov brought trees and planted them in Egypt, telling his children to cut them down and bring them out when they left Egypt.16 Only through such advance preparations were these raw materials available. This midrash implies that there were always plans to build a Mishkan! Had Rashi maintained that the Mishkan was a *bedieved* scenario, why would Bnei Yisrael have taken these large trees out of Egypt before ever needing a Mishkan? The Chizkuni and Ibn Ezra on *Shemos* 25:5 both refer to alternative sources through which Bnei Yisrael acquired this wood while already in the desert, ones which Rashi could have easily adopted.

Perhaps we can suggest an approach to Rashi's method that lies somewhere between the approaches of the Sforno and the Ramban. There was always a plan to have a Mishkan in the desert, with a limited role. Our *Avos* provided a wooden framework in the form of *atzei shittim* (and perhaps, deliberately, nothing else). However, the specific contents and roles within were to be dictated by the needs of Klal Yisrael at the time. After the *chet ha'eigel*, it became clear that a great part of the Mishkan's construction and daily *avodah* would need to serve as a *kapparah*. As the *Midrash Rabbah* states (*Shemos* 48:6):

מָה כְּתִיב בְּאוֹתָהּ קַלְקָלָה? 'פָּרְקוּ נִזְמֵי הַזָּהָב'. וּמָה הֵבִיאוּ? נְזָמִים.

What is written in that [calamity of the *eigel*]? They removed their golden rings [for the purposes of melting them into the *eigel*]. And what did they bring [for the construction of the Mishkan]? Rings.

Each item within the Mishkan had a specific role in the *teshuvah* process. And even further, as explained by Rabbi Yosef Dov Soloveitchik, each donation served as an act of tzedakah, a central element in the *teshuvah* process, at a unique time in history when there were no individual poor people with unfulfilled personal needs.

_____

16. The Midrash elaborates further that these trees were in fact the *eishel* that Avraham planted in Beer Sheva and that Yaakov replanted in Egypt.

This first truly communal initiative serves as a lesson to Klal Yisrael for generations. Our circumstances and needs change over the course of Jewish history. At each of these junctures we must adapt, seeking opportunities to remain selflessly devoted to the *klal* and to one another, while firmly anchored within the confines of the beautiful *mesorah* of our *Avos* who have led before us.

· פרשת ויקרא ·

PARASHAS VAYIKRA

KORBANOS: NOT MUCH OF A SACRIFICE

BY RABBI ELIYAHU RAPOPORT

דַּבֵּר אֶל בְּנֵי יִשְׂרָאֵל וְאָמַרְתָּ אֲלֵהֶם אָדָם כִּי יַקְרִיב מִכֶּם קָרְבָּן לַה' מִן הַבְּהֵמָה מִן הַבָּקָר וּמִן הַצֹּאן תַּקְרִיבוּ אֶת קָרְבַּנְכֶם. (ויקרא א, ב)

Speak to the children of Israel and say to them: When any of you present an offering of cattle to Hashem, he shall choose his offering from the herd or from the flock. (*Vayikra* 1:2)

אָמַר רַבִּי אַסִּי, מִפְּנֵי מָה מַתְחִילִין לַתִּינוֹקוֹת בְּתוֹרַת כֹּהֲנִים וְאֵין מַתְחִילִין בִּבְרֵאשִׁית, אֶלָּא שֶׁהַתִּינוֹקוֹת טְהוֹרִין וְהַקָּרְבָּנוֹת טְהוֹרִין, יָבוֹאוּ טְהוֹרִין וְיִתְעַסְּקוּ בַּטְּהוֹרִים. (ויקרא רבה ז, ג)

Rabbi Asi said: Why do we begin teaching young children with *Sefer Vayikra*, and not *Sefer Bereishis*? Because young children are pure, and sacrifices are pure—let the pure ones come and involve themselves in pure subjects. (*Vayikra Rabbah* 7:3)

Sefer Vayikra, the book of *korbanos*, holds center stage, both literally, as the third of the five books of the Torah, as well as figuratively, with *korbanos* being so central to our relationship with Hashem.

Early in our history, at the Bris bein Habesarim, Hashem told Avraham Avinu that it was the merit of the *korbanos* that would maintain our connection to Eretz Yisrael. When the Rambam describes the accomplishments Mashiach will achieve, he talks of the restoration of *korbanos*. What is it about *korbanos* that is so integral to Judaism and that we so yearn for Mashiach to reinstate?

The Gemara (*Menachos* 110a) tells us that *korbanos* accomplish more for us than they do for He to Whom they are offered:

וְשֶׁמָּא תֹּאמַר: לַאֲכִילָה הוּא צָרִיךָ, תַּלְמוּד לוֹמַר 'אִם אֶרְעַב לֹא אֹמַר
לָךְ כִּי לִי תֵבֵל וּמְלוֹאָהּ', וְנֶאֱמַר 'כִּי לִי כָל חַיְתוֹ יָעַר בְּהֵמוֹת בְּהַרְרֵי אָלֶף
יָדַעְתִּי כָּל עוֹף הָרִים וְזִיז שָׂדַי עִמָּדִי הַאוֹכַל בְּשַׂר אַבִּירִים וְדַם עַתּוּדִים
אֶשְׁתֶּה', לֹא אָמַרְתִּי אֲלֵיכֶם: זִבְחוּ כְּדֵי שֶׁתֹּאמַר אֶעֱשֶׂה רְצוֹנוֹ וְיַעֲשֶׂה
רְצוֹנִי, לֹא לִרְצוֹנִי אַתֶּם זוֹבְחִים אֶלָּא לִרְצוֹנְכֶם אַתֶּם זוֹבְחִים, שֶׁנֶּאֱמַר
'לִרְצוֹנְכֶם תִּזְבָּחֻהוּ'.

And lest you say that Hashem needs these offerings for consumption, the *pasuk* states: "If I were hungry, I would not tell you; for the world is Mine, and everything within it" (*Tehillim* 50:12). And it is stated: "For every beast of the forest is Mine, and the cattle upon a thousand hills. I know all the fowls of the mountains; and the wild beasts of the field are Mine" (ibid. 50:10–11). Similarly, it is stated in the following *pasuk*: "Do I eat the flesh of bulls, or drink the blood of goats?" (ibid. 50:13). I did not say to you: Sacrifice offerings to me, so that you will say: "I will do His will, i.e., fulfill His needs, and He will do my will." You are not sacrificing to fulfill My will, i.e., My needs, but you are sacrificing to fulfill your will, as it is stated: "And when you sacrifice an offering of peace offerings to Hashem, you shall sacrifice it so that you may be accepted" (*Vayikra* 19:5).

Perhaps echoing this gemara, Rabbi Samson Raphael Hirsch (on *Vayikra* 1:2) bemoans the inadequacy of the commonly given translation of the word *korban*. This inadequacy, he argues, leads to a warped perspective of what *korbanos* are all about. In his words:

It is most regrettable that we have no word which really repro-
duces the idea which lies in the word קרבן. The unfortunate use
of the term "sacrifice" implies the idea of giving something up
that is of value to oneself for the benefit of another...which is
not only entirely absent from the nature and the idea of a קרבן
but are diametrically opposed to it [emphasis added]...

קרב means to approach, to come near and into a close relationship with someone... The idea of and purpose of הקרבה is the
attainment of a higher sphere of life. It thus rejects both the idea
of a sacrifice, of giving something up, of losing something, as
well as of its being a requirement of the One to Whom one gets
near... The מקריב desires that something of himself should come
into closer relationship to Hashem... It is קרבת אלקים which is
striven for by a קרבן...which for a Jew is the highest, yea, the
only conception of what is "good."17

Our Sages tell us that in the absence of a Beis Hamikdash our *tefillos*
take the place of *korbanos*. This is taken so literally that it is the *korbanos* which determine the exact timing of the *Shacharis, Minchah, and
Ma'ariv* prayers. In fact, our purity of thought, degree of concentration,
and meticulousness in our behavior and dress during *tefillah* are all dictated by the halachos of *korbanos* (*Shulchan Aruch, Orach Chaim* 98:4):

הַתְּפִלָּה הִיא בִּמְקוֹם הַקָּרְבָּן, וּלְכָךְ צָרִיךְ לִזָּהֵר לְזָהֵר שֶׁתְּהֵא דֻּגְמַת הַקָּרְבָּן
בְּכַוָּנָה וְלֹא יְעָרֵב בָּהּ מַחֲשָׁבָה אַחֶרֶת, כְּמוֹ מַחֲשָׁבָה שֶׁפּוֹסֶלֶת בְּקָדָשִׁים;
וּמְעֻמָּד, דֻּומְיָא דַעֲבוֹדָה; קְבִיעוּת מָקוֹם כְּמוֹ הַקָּרְבָּנוֹת, שֶׁכָּל אֶחָד קָבוּעַ
מְקוֹמוֹ לִשְׁחִיטָתוֹ וּמַתַּן דָּמָיו; וְשֶׁלֹּא יָחוּץ דָּבָר בֵּינוֹ לַקִּיר, דֻּומְיָא דְּקָרְבָּן
שֶׁהַחֲצִיצָה פּוֹסֶלֶת בֵּינוֹ לַכְּלִי; וְרָאוּי שֶׁיִּהְיוּ לוֹ מַלְבּוּשִׁים נָאִים מְיֻחָדִים
לַתְּפִלָּה, כְּגוֹן בִּגְדֵי כְהֻנָּה, אֶלָּא שֶׁאֵין כָּל אָדָם יָכוֹל לְבַזְבֵּז עַל זֶה, וּמִכָּל
מָקוֹם טוֹב הוּא שֶׁיִּהְיוּ לוֹ מִכְנָסַיִם מְיֻחָדִים לַתְּפִלָּה, מִשּׁוּם נְקִיּוּת.

17. Rabbi Samson Raphael Hirsch, *The Pentateuch* (New York: Judaica Press, 1971).

Prayer is in place of sacrifices, and therefore one must be careful to follow the format of sacrifices with respect to intention,
and not let other thoughts mix in, similar to unrelated thoughts
which would nullify sacrifices. And prayer must be recited standing, like the service in the Temple; and in a fixed place like the
sacrifices, where each one had a fixed place for its slaughter and
the sprinkling of its blood; and that nothing should separate
between one and the wall [during prayer], similar to sacrifices
where any separation between it and the vessel would nullify
it; and it is appropriate that one should have special, nice garments for prayer, like the clothing of the *kohanim*, though understandably not everyone can spend the money on this; and
in any case it is appropriate to have special pants for prayer, for
the sake of cleanliness.

Perhaps it is no coincidence, then, that the true meaning of the word *tefillah* is also lost in translation. As the Lubavitcher Rebbe says, the common translation of the word, which is "prayer," completely misses the
mark. He explains that "prayer" in Hebrew is not *tefillah* but *bakashah*.
And these terms are opposites. *Bakashah* means to pray, request, be-
seech. But *tefillah* means to attach oneself. Through *bakashah* the person
asks Hashem to provide him, from Above, with what he lacks. Therefore, when he is not in need of anything, or feels no desire for a gift
from Above, *bakashah* becomes redundant.

Through *tefillah*, by contrast, the person seeks to attach himself to
Hashem. It is a movement from below, from man, reaching toward Him.
This is something appropriate to everyone and at every time. The Jewish
neshamah has a bond with Hashem, but it also inhabits a body, whose
preoccupation with the material world may attenuate that bond. So it has
to constantly be strengthened and renewed. This is the function of *tefillah*, and it is necessary for every Jew. For while there may be those who
do not lack anything and thus have nothing to request of Hashem, there
is no one who does not need to attach himself to the Source of all life.

Thus, the *avodah* of *korbanos* and the *avodah* of *tefillah* are in a sense one and the same. They are both about becoming close to and connecting with Hashem, about coming to recognize and identify with our *neshamah*, which yearns to reach beyond the confines of our material existence and to connect and be in tune with its Creator.

This *avodah* can be a challenge. The *Zohar* says that *"she'as tzelosa she'as kerava,"* tefillah is a time of battle. We naturally feel distracted and sometimes frustrated as we try to focus our thoughts and harness our emotions toward Hashem in prayer. It is a process that requires consistent hard work and determination as we exert ourselves to overcome these obstacles and engage our minds and hearts. But when Mashiach comes, all of this will change. The pursuit of materialism will no longer be so compelling to us. Perhaps, then, we can say that the *yom shekulo Shabbos u'menuchah*, the day to come of eternal Shabbos and rest, will also be a *yom shekulo tefillah*, day of complete *tefillah*, a year-round Yom Kippur. In the words of the Rambam (*Mishneh Torah, Hilchos Teshuvah* 9:2), at that time our sole preoccupation will be the knowledge of Hashem:

וּמִפְּנֵי זֶה נִתְאַוּוּ כָּל יִשְׂרָאֵל נְבִיאֵיהֶם וְחַכְמֵיהֶם לִימוֹת הַמָּשִׁיחַ ... לְפִי שֶׁבְּאוֹתָן הַיָּמִים תַּרְבֶּה הַדֵּעָה וְהַחָכְמָה וְהָאֱמֶת, שֶׁנֶּאֱמַר 'כִּי מָלְאָה הָאָרֶץ דֵּעָה אֶת ה'', וְנֶאֱמַר 'וְלֹא יְלַמְּדוּ אִישׁ אֶת אָחִיו וְאִישׁ אֶת רֵעֵהוּ', וְנֶאֱמַר 'וַהֲסִרֹתִי אֶת לֵב הָאֶבֶן מִבְּשַׂרְכֶם'.

Because of this, all of Israel, their prophets, and their scholars craved for the messianic era... For in those days, knowledge and wisdom and truth will increase, as it is stated: "For the earth shall be full of the knowledge of Hashem" (*Yeshayahu* 11:9); and it is again stated: "And they shall teach no more every man his neighbor, and every man his brother" (*Yirmiyahu* 31:33); and it is yet again stated: "And I will take the stony heart out of your flesh" (*Yechezkel* 36:26).

This is the reason we yearn for Mashiach, and it is this that will find expression in the reinstating of *korbanos*. May we indeed merit to see the fulfillment of the *pasuk* in *Yechezkel* (ibid.):

וְנָתַתִּי לָכֶם לֵב חָדָשׁ וְרוּחַ חֲדָשָׁה אֶתֵּן בְּקִרְבְּכֶם וַהֲסִרֹתִי אֶת לֵב הָאֶבֶן מִבְּשַׂרְכֶם וְנָתַתִּי לָכֶם לֵב בָּשָׂר.

And I will give you a new heart and put a new spirit into you, and I will remove the heart of stone from your body and give you a heart of flesh.

· פרשת צו ·

PARASHAS TZAV

NIGHT VERSUS DAY

BY RABBI DR. JOSH DREDZE

In *Parashas Tzav*, the Torah continues presenting laws of *korbanos*, and concludes its presentation with the following words (*Vayikra* 7:37–38):

זֹאת הַתּוֹרָה ... אֲשֶׁר צִוָּה ה' אֶת מֹשֶׁה בְּהַר סִינָי בְּיוֹם צַוֹּתוֹ אֶת בְּנֵי יִשְׂרָאֵל לְהַקְרִיב אֶת קָרְבְּנֵיהֶם לַה' בְּמִדְבַּר סִינָי.

This is the law...which Hashem commanded Moshe at Har Sinai, on the day Hashem commanded the children of Israel.

In his commentary to an earlier passage in *Sefer Vayikra* (6:2), Rabbi Samson Raphael Hirsch discusses the nature of day and night, and why the Torah emphasizes that Hashem gave these laws specifically during the day. Rabbi Hirsch explains that day is a period of clarity and free will, and a state of wakefulness, while night is a time of confusion, and is more physical in nature. He therefore suggests that Hashem gave the laws of *korbanos* during the day so that people would engage in Him through the *korbanos* while in their peak state, when they were most clearheaded—similar to Moshe's state when he received prophecy *peh el peh*, from one mouth to another (*Bamidbar* 12:8; unlike other prophets, who received prophecy in a less direct, dreamlike state).

Rabbi Hirsch says that, for the same reason, the Torah commands that the *korbanos* themselves must be offered during the daytime (also learned from *Vayikra* 7:37; see *Megillah* 20b, Rashi there). Daytime is when people are at their optimal, most clearheaded state, and therefore best suited to engage with Hashem.

Rabbi Hirsch, however, points out a seeming inconsistency with this explanation, from the beginning of the parashah. Earlier in the *parashah* (*Vayikra* 6:2), the Torah says that the *korban olah* was to be "*mokdah al hamizbei'ach kol halaylah*—burning on the fire the entire night." If the optimal time for *korbanos* and a person's *avodah* is during the day, then why is the *olah* burned at night?

Rabbi Hirsch answers that the daytime requirement referred specifically to the procedure of offering the *korbanos* (the *semichah*, leaning; *shechitah*, slaughtering; *kemitzah*, separating; etc.). Due to its stated goal of effecting *kapparah*, and a renewal with Hashem and His Torah, the offering itself had to be done when people were in peak form, i.e., during the day. In the case of burning the *olah*, however, the *kapparah* was already achieved during the daytime. The Torah then commands that the *olah* be burned at night, to stress that *kapparah* and *hakravah*, the bringing of the *korban* on the altar, had already occurred. It was specifically the fact that the *olah* was already offered during the day which enabled it to be burned at night. Rabbi Hirsch further states that, in this way, "*halaylah holech achar hayom*—night follows day," meaning that our ability to function at night depends on our achievements of the preceding day.

Rabbi Hirsch's conception of day and night extends beyond *korbanos*. In our *avodas Hashem*, and in our lives in general, our ability to grow and worship during the clearer times of daylight enables us to continue to engage during the nighttime as well. Rabbi Hirsch is teaching us that during difficult times, we must draw on those achievements attained during brighter, more optimal moments. While periods of darkness are inevitable and inherently more difficult, if we grow and seek Hashem when times are clearer, we will be better equipped to engage and serve Him even during more ambiguous and challenging times.

· פרשת שמיני ·

PARASHAS SHEMINI

TRUST THE SOFRIM: EMUNAS CHACHAMIM

BY RABBI AARON FEIGENBAUM

The Gemara in *Kiddushin* (30a) says that in *Parashas Shemini* we reach the midway point of the Torah for letters and for *pesukim*. The Gemara says that the early generations were called *Sofrim* because they kept exact counts of the Torah. They calculated that the letter *vav* in the word *gachon* (*Vayikra* 11:42) is the halfway point for letters in the Torah, and that the words *darosh darash* (ibid. 10:16) are the halfway point for words in the Torah.

The problem is that our Torah has 304,805 letters, half of which would be 152,402.5, and the *vav* of *gachon* is letter 157,236, about 5,000 letters after the midpoint of letters in the Torah. The words also don't work out. Our Torah has 79,980 words, half of which is 39,990, and the words *darosh darash* are words 40,921 and 40,922, about 1,000 words after the midpoint.

If this wasn't bad enough, the Gemara continues that there are 5,888 *pesukim* in the Torah, but in fact our Torah has only 5,845 *pesukim*. It would seem that we are left with two choices: Either we are missing 43 *pesukim*, or these *Sofrim* were not such impressive counters after all.

Rabbi Menachem Mendel Kasher, *zt"l*, records a theory from Rabbi Yitzchak Yosef Zilber, *zt"l*, that indeed our Torah has only 5,845 *pesukim*, but there are eight times in *Tehillim* and thirty-five times in *Divrei Hayamim* that *pesukim* from the *Chumash* are repeated word for word. Adding these 43 *pesukim*, we arrive at the count of the *Sofrim* of 5,888 *pesukim* in the Torah.

As for the letters of the Torah, Rabbi Zilber suggests that the *Sofrim* were not counting letters; anyone can count letters, for it does not take any special wisdom or knowledge. The *Sofrim* were teaching that there are letters in the Torah that tradition tells us to write larger or smaller. There are seventeen such letters in the Torah, and the *vav* of *gachon*, written larger, is the ninth of these letters, exactly in the middle, with eight large and small letters before it and eight after it.

Finally, as for the words, the *Sofrim* were not just counting the words of the Torah. There are seventy-seven times when the Torah uses double words (for example, "Avraham, Avraham") and *darosh darash* is the thirty-ninth time, exactly in the middle, with thirty-eight doubled words before and thirty-eight after.

This is a remarkable explanation of the Gemara, but it indicates two additional lessons. First, the proficiency of the *Sofrim* is awesome and inspiring. Without any forms of technology they not only mastered the text of the Torah, but they also knew precisely all of the anomalies of the text, repeated *pesukim*, larger and smaller letters, and doubled words. Second, this reinforces a sense of *emunas chachamim*. It would have been easy to learn the Gemara in *Kiddushin* and see that all of the calculations were wrong and either dismiss the Sages as fools, or worse, dismiss the Torah as we have it as incomplete. The truth, meanwhile, is that the Sages were correct and the Torah we have is perfect; we just didn't understand the formula they were using. We often see only part of the picture, and it sometimes takes centuries for someone to uncover the truth behind a statement of the Sages. Until we see the whole picture we can maintain a strong sense of *emunah* in Hashem, in our Torah, and in our Sages.

· פרשת תזריע ·

PARASHAS TAZRIA

KEEPING OUR PERSPECTIVE
ON KEDUSHAH

BY DANIEL WEISS

Parashas Tazria details the laws of *tumas yoledes*, the *tumah* of a woman who gives birth. The Torah's description of a woman becoming pregnant, *tazria* (*Vayikra* 12:1), is unique. This verb's only other appearances in *Tanach* are in *Bereishis* 1:11 and 1:12, where the Torah describes the vegetation that Hashem created on the third day of Creation as "*eisev mazria zera*—grass producing seeds." Associating the reproduction of plants with human reproduction is somewhat surprising, as they are very different. For man, reproduction is a long process. He has to seek a spouse whom he shares a common vision and identity with. He has to create the proper environment to nurture and raise his children. By contrast, the reproduction of plants is much simpler and happens freely and sporadically.

Rabbi Samson Raphael Hirsch, in his commentary on *Chumash* (*Vayikra* 12:2), explains that by alluding to the mother's role in producing progeny in a "purely material physical character,"[18] the Torah is explaining the source for the *tumas yoledes* described in this parashah. The term *tazria* is suggesting that man grows no differently than a plant. Reproduction is a natural process. It is devoid of the higher subliminal message that the Torah has for mankind and is therefore a source of *tumah*. It is precisely for this reason that the Torah needs to reestablish the identity of man as being distinctly different from that of a plant. Man has free will, which

---

18. Rabbi Samson Raphael Hirsch, *The Pentateuch* (New York: Judaica Press, 1971).

is used to choose between Hashem's intended path and the darkness of those who forsake it. The *korban* offered by the *yoledes* restores the balance that the Torah wants of man being *kadosh*. "The mother herself, under the fresh impression of her physically, completely passively and painfully having to submit to the forces of the physical laws of nature at the most sublime procedure of her earthly calling, has to reestablish again the consciousness of her own spiritual height."[19]

This idea is noteworthy in several regards. It shows us a technique that Rabbi Hirsch uses frequently, that in order to understand a word in the Torah, we need to trace it back to its origin. In this case, the word *tazria* is understood more completely by tracing it back to its original appearance in *Bereishis*. This is also an example of how the Torah empowers man to establish balance in life between worldly matters and spiritual matters. Through acts of *kedushah*, man maintains perspective on holiness.

We do many mitzvos in our daily life, many of which provide an opportunity to restore the balance we need to keep our perspective on *kedushah*. We need to put greater emphasis on the *kedushah* inherent in mitzvos performed in the context of more physical actions.

For example, the Sages instituted a mitzvah to wash our hands before eating bread. This *takanah* was made so that when we merit the return of the Beis Hamikdash, the *kohanim* will be accustomed to washing their hands before partaking of *terumah*.[20] This mitzvah can mistakenly be viewed as geared toward a specific class, and irrelevant to the Jewish nation in its present state when there is no partaking of *terumah*. However, when viewed properly, it's a tremendous opportunity to elevate ourselves by transforming our meals into models of *kedushah*. Washing gives us a glimpse into the future; it enables us to practice for a future time when Mashiach will be here together with the glory of the Beis Hamikdash, *korbanos*, and *terumah*.

---

19. Rabbi Samson Raphael Hirsch, *The Pentateuch* (New York: Judaica Press, 1971).
20. See *Mishnah Berurah* 158:1, as well as an additional reason cited there.

That our Sages saw fit to enact this *takanah* brings to light that our *geulah* will come very quickly and that we will be caught off guard by it, and therefore need to actively prepare ourselves now. There won't be time to produce halachic guidance literature like the works on *kashrus*, Shabbos, and *berachos* that we benefit from today. Therefore the Sages had no choice other than to enact the *takanah* of washing before bread to enable us to practice, knowing that the *geulah sheleimah* will be so sudden that this is the only way to ensure the proper observance of the mitzvah. May we merit to use our opportunities to actively prepare ourselves for the *geulah sheleimah*. May we also merit that the redemption comes speedily and catches us off guard, despite our preparations for its coming.

· פרשת מצורע ·

PARASHAS METZORA

TWO TYPES OF ISOLATION: METZORA AND THE KOHEN GADOL

BY RABBI YEHUDA TURETSKY

While individuals are obligated in numerous mitzvos, many of them can be fulfilled only in the presence of others. The Gemara (*Megillah* 23b) tells us that absent a halachic *tzibbur*, we are unable to fulfill certain halachos. Indeed, a variety of obligations are incumbent not on an individual, but rather on the Jewish people as a whole. In that sense, the Torah clearly desires us to function as part of a community and not merely as individuals.

Given the Torah's perspective on the necessity of community, it is most surprising that halachah requires certain individuals to undergo periods of isolation. Indeed, two individuals are obligated to separate themselves from society: The *metzora* must be alone and cut off from society until he becomes pure, and the *kohen gadol* is required to isolate himself for a week prior to performing the Yom Kippur *avodah*. If being around others is so critical, though, why are they required to be apart from others? Why are they not permitted to be surrounded by the community deemed so critical in halachah?

Rabbi Samson Raphael Hirsch in his commentary on the Torah (*Vayikra* 13:59) proves that the *metzora* is isolated not because he has a contagious illness. Indeed, there is minimal evidence that we treat the *metzora* as someone whose physical symptoms can impact others. Rather, as Rashi (ibid.) quotes from the Gemara (*Arachin* 16b), the *metzora* caused rifts and discord among individuals by speaking *lashon hara*; it is only appropriate then that he be isolated in return (see *Seridei Eish*

1:171). For the *metzora*, therefore, part of isolation may be not only a punishment, but also part of a larger process of *teshuvah*. The *metzora* goes through a lengthy purification process (*Vayikra* 14), and a lot of it may be geared toward allowing him to appreciate the impact of his actions so that he can better prepare himself to reenter society. For that reason, the *metzora* must be alone, because only by being alone can he come to recognize the nature of his actions and what is required of him when he is around others. The Torah wishes us to be part of a society, but only when we are deemed worthy, not when we create divisiveness.

The *kohen gadol* must also be isolated, but for a different reason. While some ambiguity exists in understanding precisely why, many suggest it is part of an intense preparatory process (see *Yoma* 2a–b and *Shiurei HaGrid*, ad loc.). Only by isolating himself temporarily can the *kohen gadol* sanctify himself to the extent needed to perform the *avodah* on Yom Kippur. The *kohen gadol*'s isolation is not a punishment, but an act of preparation on behalf of others; he focuses intensely for one week to make himself worthy and to able to provide for the Jewish people the atonement they hope to achieve on Yom Kippur.

For the *metzora*, isolation is a punishment, geared toward ensuring that he no longer be a destructive force in society. By contrast, for the *kohen gadol*, isolation allows him to best prepare to support and provide for the Jewish people on Yom Kippur.

Communal life strengthens us and allows us to fully embrace a life predicated on values of *emunah* in Hashem. Yet there are specific situations where only through being alone can we best strengthen and prepare ourselves to effectively participate in and contribute to Jewish life. As such, the benefits of community can and should never be taken for granted. Community can provide us with so much love, support, and care, and we hope to be worthy of its embrace and to add to its awesome power.

· פרשת אחרי מות ·

PARASHAS ACHAREI MOS

BEZOS YAVO AHARON EL HAKODESH

BY DR. DOVID KRAUSZ

Parashas Acharei Mos begins with Hashem commanding Moshe Rabbeinu regarding the proper *avodah* that Aharon Hakohen was to perform when entering the Kodesh Hakodashim. There are numerous *pesukim* (*Vayikra*, ch. 16) devoted to the Yom Kippur *avodah*; the Torah lists the order of the day by describing the various *korbanos*, lottery, *ketores* service, and immersions that the *kohen gadol* was to perform.

One of the prominent parts of the Yom Kippur rituals involved the *kohen gadol* changing between his gold and linen garments to perform the various parts of the *avodah*. Each time he changed his clothing, he purified in a *mikveh* before donning new clothes. There is an oral tradition (*halachah leMoshe miSinai*) which dictates that on Yom Kippur, the *kohel gadol* immersed in the *mikveh* five times (*Yoma* 32a).

However, a careful reading of our *pesukim* reveals that the *kohen gadol* changed his garments (and therefore immersed in the *mikveh*) only three times! How do we reconcile the tradition of five immersions with the *pesukim* here?

There is a further oddity noted in conjunction with these *pesukim* pointed out by Rabbi Yehuda Cooperman, *zt"l*, in his *sefer Peshuto shel Mikra*. Typically, when the Torah introduces a Yom Tov and its associated *avodah* and mandates, it first names the Yom Tov and then continues to describe its features. See, for example, *Parashas Emor* (*Vayikra* 23:27), where the Torah introduces Yom Kippur and then outlines the relevant laws. In our case, however, we find the opposite: First the Torah describes the details of the *avodah* of Yom Kippur, and only then are we told (ibid. 16:29):

וְהָיְתָה לָכֶם לְחֻקַּת עוֹלָם בַּחֹדֶשׁ הַשְּׁבִיעִי בֶּעָשׂוֹר לַחֹדֶשׁ תְּעַנּוּ אֶת נַפְשֹׁתֵיכֶם.

And it will be to you a decree forever in the seventh month on the tenth of the month, you shall afflict your souls.

Why do we see a deviation from the normal pattern?

To resolve the discrepancy between our tradition of five immersions and the *peshat* of the *pesukim* in our parashah, Rashi explains that our *pesukim* are ordered to reflect the sequence of events regarding the *avodah* of the *kohen gadol* on Yom Kippur, with the exception of one *pasuk* (ibid. 16:23):

וּבָא אַהֲרֹן אֶל אֹהֶל מוֹעֵד וּפָשַׁט אֶת בִּגְדֵי הַבָּד אֲשֶׁר לָבַשׁ בְּבֹאוֹ אֶל הַקֹּדֶשׁ וְהִנִּיחָם שָׁם.

And Aharon will come into the *Ohel Mo'ed* and remove the linen clothes that he wore when he came into the holy [place] and he will place them there.

Rashi's assertion is based on the Gemara in *Yoma* (32a):

'וּבָא אַהֲרֹן אֶל אֹהֶל מוֹעֵד'. לָמָה הוּא בָּא? אֵינוּ בָּא אֶלָּא לְהוֹצִיא אֶת הַכַּף וְאֶת הַמַּחְתָּה, (שֶׁכָּל) הַפָּרָשָׁה כֻּלָּהּ נֶאֶמְרָה עַל הַסֵּדֶר חוּץ מִפָּסוּק זֶה. מַאי טַעְמָא? אָמַר רַב חִסְדָּא, גְּמִירֵי חָמֵשׁ טְבִילוֹת וַעֲשָׂרָה קִדּוּשִׁין טוֹבֵל כֹּהֵן גָּדוֹל וּמְקַדֵּשׁ בּוֹ בַּיּוֹם, וְאִי כְּסִדְרָן, לֹא מַשְׁכַּחַת לְהוּ אֶלָּא שָׁלֹשׁ טְבִילוֹת וְשִׁשָּׁה קִדּוּשִׁין.

"And Aharon will come into the *Ohel Mo'ed*." Why does he come? His purpose is to remove the spoon and pan, as (the entire) parashah is written in proper order except for this verse. Why [do we assert this]? Rabbi Chisda says, we have a tradition that five immersions [in the *mikveh*] and ten sanctifications [of the hands through handwashing] the *kohen gadol* does that day. If we were to assume that the *pesukim* are written in the proper order, it would come out that there are only three immersions and six sanctifications.

Rashi explains that this *pasuk* should actually appear after the *kohen gadol* sacrifices his and the nation's ram *olah* offerings, which would thereby require him to shed his gold garments, immerse, don his linen garments, remove the *ketores* ladle and shovel from the Kodesh Hakodashim, and then immerse again before changing back into his gold garments. If we transpose these actions into the correct Yom Kippur sequence, we clearly see an additional two immersions for a total of five.

Rashi's explanation based on the Gemara works well to resolve the discrepancy of the number of immersions, but begs a further question: Why does the Torah describe the *avodah* out of sequence? What can we learn from the simple *peshat* reading of the *pesukim*?

To understand the deeper meaning here, we must jump back to the beginning of our parashah. *Parashas Acharei Mos* opens with Hashem's directive to Moshe to relay to Aharon the severity of entering the Kodesh Hakodashim (*Vayikra* 16:2):

וַיֹּאמֶר ה' אֶל מֹשֶׁה דַּבֵּר אֶל אַהֲרֹן אָחִיךָ וְאַל יָבֹא בְכָל עֵת אֶל הַקֹּדֶשׁ מִבֵּית לַפָּרֹכֶת אֶל פְּנֵי הַכַּפֹּרֶת אֲשֶׁר עַל הָאָרֹן וְלֹא יָמוּת.

And Hashem said to Moshe: "Tell Aharon your brother not to come into the [inner holy chamber] at any time, inside the curtain, facing the cover which is on the Ark, to prevent yourself from perishing."

Interestingly, the Midrash tells us that Moshe Rabbeinu was disturbed by Hashem's command to Aharon; he worried that the imprecision of the word *es*, time, left room for interpretation, which could, *chas veshalom*, cause Aharon to inadvertently err. The Midrash continues that

Hashem calmed Moshe by explaining that Aharon's entry into the Kodesh Hakodashim was not restricted to specific times; rather, he could enter at any time he pleased, provided that he performed the prescribed *avodah* (*Vayikra Rabbah* 21:7):

וְאַל יָבֹא בְכָל עֵת, אָמַר רַבִּי יְהוּדָה בְּרַבִּי סִימוֹן, צַעַר גָּדוֹל הָיָה לוֹ לְמשֶׁה בַּדָּבָר זֶה, אָמַר אוֹי לִי שֶׁמָּא נִדְחַף אָחִי אַהֲרֹן מִמְּחִצָּתוֹ ... אָמַר הַקָּדוֹשׁ בָּרוּךְ הוּא לְמשֶׁה לֹא כְּשֵׁם שֶׁאַתָּה סָבוּר, לֹא עֵת לְשָׁעָה, וְלֹא עֵת לְיוֹם, וְלֹא עֵת לְשָׁנָה, וְלֹא עֵת לִשְׁתֵּים עֶשְׂרֵה שָׁנָה, וְלֹא עֵת לְשִׁבְעִים שָׁנָה, וְלֹא עֵת לְעוֹלָם, אֶלָּא בְּכָל שָׁעָה שֶׁהוּא רוֹצֶה לְכָּנֵס יִכָּנֵס, רַק שֶׁיִּכָּנֵס בַּסֵּדֶר הַזֶּה.

"Do not come at any time." Rabbi Yehudah the son of Rabbi Shimon explains: Moshe had a lot of anguish over this [injunction], thinking: "Woe is me that perhaps Aharon my brother is being pushed away from the [inner circle of Hashem]" ... Hakadosh Baruch Hu said to Moshe, "It is not as you are thinking. [The injunction of not coming in at] 'any time' is not [prohibiting entering during a particular] hour, nor a day, nor a year, nor twelve years, nor seventy years. Rather, whenever he wants to he can enter! However, when he comes in, he must come in with this order."

From there, the Torah proceeds to describe what that *avodah* entailed: It would allow Aharon Hakohen to enter the Kodesh Hakodashim at any time.

Therein lies the beauty of the *kipeshuto* reading of our *pesukim*. It is highlighted by Rabbi Cooperman in *Peshuto shel Mikra*, where he quotes the *Chochmas Adam*, who quotes the Gra on this midrash. The *pesukim* at face value describe the *avodah* necessary for entering the Kodesh Hakodashim on a daily basis—which would require only three immersions!

A simple reading of the *pesukim* resolves both mysteries. We can understand the apparent misordering of the *pesukim*: The primary focus of this set of *pesukim* is the description of *avodah* requirements for regular daily entry into the Kodesh Hakodashim. Further, we now recognize why the Torah deviates from its normal pattern of naming the Yom Tov before describing the *avodah*: Since the initial description was not inherently tied to Yom Kippur, the Torah mentions the Yom Tov only afterward, along with additional mandates of the day.

Does this allowance of entry into the Kodesh Hakodashim apply just to Aharon Hakohen, or is it permitted for all *kohanim gedolim* throughout the generations? The Meshech Chochmah interprets our *pesukim* as pertaining specifically to the generation of the wilderness, thereby allowing Aharon and subsequently his son Elazar Hakohen to enter at any time. He quotes the Sforno to elucidate the distinction between the *kohanim gedolim* in the desert and future *kohanim gedolim*.

The Sforno highlights that while the Menorah in the Beis Hamikdash was lit by any *kohen*, the *kohen gadol* himself lit the Menorah in the Mishkan during the forty years in the desert. The reason for this, he explains, is that during those years the Shechinah was in the Mishkan at all times. The Meshech Chochmah extrapolates from the Sforno that it was precisely the continuous presence of the Shechinah that allowed for the *kohen gadol* to enter the Kodesh Hakodashim at any time.

The Meshech Chochmah says further that there is another reason to allow the *kohen gadol* in the desert to enter the Kodesh Hakodashim throughout the year. In two separate instances, the *pasuk* says that the *avodos* were performed to purify Bnei Yisrael: "*Vechiper…mitumos Bnei Yisrael*—He will atone…for the impurities of the children of Israel" (*Vayikra* 16:16) and "*Vechiper es Mikdash Hakodesh…veal kol am hakahal yechapeir*—He will atone for the Holy of Holies…and on all the congregation he will atone" (ibid. 16:33). These statements are referring to *tumas Mikdash vekodoshav* (*Shevuos* 7a), meaning, the bringing of *korbanos* to atone for any *tumah* brought into the Beis Hamikdash or eating *korbanos* in a state of *tumah*. In the times of the Mishkan, the Jewish people were not allowed to eat *basar taavah*, meat for the sake of nonsacrificial purposes, and because of this they ate *basar kodesh* regularly. Since this meant there was increased traffic passing through the Mishkan, there was an elevated risk of *tumah* entering the *Mikdash*; therefore, they needed more atonement. This is the reason Aharon Hakohen could go into the Kodesh Hakodashim at any time: to atone for the extra *tumas Mikdash vekodoshav*. It therefore follows that this reason would continue to apply after Aharon Hakohen's death once Elazar took over as *kohen gadol*, since the ban on *basar ta'avah* still applied.

Rabbi Cooperman concludes by positing his view on how these halachos will manifest at the time of the third and final Beis Hamikdash. He quotes the Kli Chemdah, who states that in the times of *techiyas hameisim*, when Moshe and Aharon return, Aharon will once again be able to enter the Kodesh Hakodashim daily to perform the *avodah*. Rabbi Cooperman adds, according to the Meshech Chochmah based on the Sforno, that the level of *kedushah* of the third Beis Hamikdash will certainly rival the *kedushah* of the Mishkan in the desert, and that this permission to enter the Kodesh Hakodashim daily will be granted to any *kohen gadol*.

May we be *zocheh* to witness these halachos in practice and bask in the presence of the Shechinah with the coming of Mashiach, *bimheirah beyameinu*.

· פרשת קדושים ·

PARASHAS KEDOSHIM

LO SIKOM

BY RABBI CHAIM TWERSKI

לֹא תִקֹּם וְלֹא תִטֹּר אֶת בְּנֵי עַמֶּךָ וְאָהַבְתָּ לְרֵעֲךָ כָּמוֹךָ אֲנִי ה'. (ויקרא יט, יח)

Do not avenge or bear a grudge against a member of your nation; you shall love your fellow as you do yourself; I am Hashem. (*Vayikra* 19:18)

The Torah seems to be giving an almost superhuman set of commands. Man is given instincts that guide him in his actions. The concept of possession, of fairness, and the desire for revenge are among them. Even a one-year-old understands possession, and very small children, including toddlers, comprehend fairness, as well as the desire for revenge when harmed. These ideas are not taught by society; they are innate to human nature.

The Torah seems to be demanding that we fight our nature—a very tall order indeed. But more difficult is that we find the Torah's promotion of vengeance as well. The *pasuk* in *Tehillim* (94:1) states, "*Keil nekamos Hashem Keil nekamos hofia*—Hashem is a God of vengeance; God of vengeance present Yourself." The Gemara (*Berachos* 33a) states, "Great is vengeance, for it was placed between two of Hashem's Names." Ironically, we even ask for revenge against our enemies every Shabbos in the *tefillah Av Harachamim* — which begins with the words "Father of Mercy"!

The halachic midrash (see *Yoma* 23a) explaining these mitzvos gives us an example of how this plays out: Reuven asks Shimon for a favor: "Lend me your hammer." Shimon refuses to do this favor. A day later,

Shimon asks Reuven for a favor: "Lend me your spade." The desire for revenge enters Reuven's heart. Under normal circumstances he would gladly lend Shimon his spade, but just yesterday Shimon refused to lend him the hammer that he needed. In his mind he says to himself, "The nerve of this man! When I ask him for a favor he turns me down, and he now has the nerve to ask me to do what he refused me just yesterday. I'd much rather give him a piece of my mind!" But the Torah demands that he go against his nature and loan him the spade nonetheless.

Next comes the question of what to say to this *mechutzaf*. The instinctive desire would be for Reuven to compare his own action with Shimon's refusal: "Yes, you can borrow my spade. I am not like you, who refused to lend me your hammer when I requested it." Here we have the Torah, which demands, "Do not bear a grudge." Instead Reuven should say, "Sure, you are welcome to it. Glad to be of service to you." In this manner friendships are created and strife is avoided. The Torah is asking us only not to be petty. By ignoring our desire for such comeuppance, we turn the wheel in the other direction, which will lead to "Love your fellow as you do yourself" (*Vayikra* 19:18).

Notice, however, that the midrash does not say to employ this mitzvah when a person does real harm to another, but only when he slights another by refusing a favor. There the line must be drawn. The Ramban states that when one party injures another, the injured party has every right and even a duty to redress the wrong, but only through a *beis din*.

What happens when a *beis din* cannot do anything due to a lack of evidence? There is a strong desire to take revenge, which will lead to an vicious cycle of violence that will never end. This is what Hillel meant when he saw the head of a murder victim floating upon the water and said (*Avos* 2:7):

עַל דַּאֲטֵפְתְּ, אַטְפוּךְ. וְסוֹף מְטִיפַיִךְ יְטוּפוּן.

It was because you drowned someone else that you were drowned, and the one who drowned you will also be drowned.

Only a *beis din* can mete out the punishment. If one takes the law into his own hands, the cycle of violence will go on and on.

In this situation one must rely upon the belief that only Hashem can administer justice. One cannot escape His justice; if it is not meted out in this world, then it will be in the next. We have the right to go to *beis din* to achieve a measure of justice, but in the final analysis, we must rely upon the true Judge and rest assured that He will repay evil with the deserved punishment.

Once we assure ourselves that justice will be done, there is no need to carry resentment in our hearts, for by doing so we damage only ourselves. Resentment in these circumstances leaves one with no peace of mind. In addition, it affects one's physical health, raising one's blood pressure and anxiety levels. We can therefore interpret these passages as applying to all situations, not just to small slights but even to major wrongs. Demanding justice through *beis din* is an approved recourse. Beyond that, have faith that Hashem will do our bidding, and try to forget the matter. It's the best course for society as a whole and for ourselves as well.

· פרשת אמור ·

PARASHAS EMOR

A KORBAN OF CHAMETZ ON SHAVUOS

BY RABBI DAVID SHER

One of the most basic rules of a *korban minchah*, a flour offering, brought in the Beis Hamikdash is that it is not permitted to become *chametz*. This rule is spelled out explicitly in *Vayikra* (2:11): "*Kol minchah asher takrivu laHashem lo sei'aseh chametz*—Any flour offering that is brought before Hashem shall not be made into leavened bread." And yet in *Parashas Emor* we are commanded to bring a *minchah chadashah*, a new flour offering, on Shavuos: the offering known as the *shtei halechem*, the two loaves of bread, which are in fact *chametz*. Other than the ten loaves brought as part of the *korban todah*, the thanksgiving offering, this is the only exception to the no-*chametz* rule. How are we to understand this exception?

In order to begin to comprehend this, we must first explain why *chametz* would be prohibited in the Beis Hamikdash in the first place. We associate *chametz* with Pesach, when it is forbidden to eat *chametz* because the bread of Bnei Yisrael did not rise during the hastened exodus from Egypt (*Shemos* 12:39). When looking more deeply at *chametz*, however, we see there is another element at play. In *Berachos* 17a, Rabbi Alexandri refers to the *yetzer hara* as the *seor sheba'isah*, the yeast in the dough. The *Sefer Hachinuch* (mitzvah 117) states that just as yeast causes dough to fill with air and rise, so too our *yetzer hara* fills us with arrogance, which causes us to ignore the words of our Creator.

We can therefore understand why in the *makom hamikdash*, where the presence of Hashem was palpable, any hint of arrogance and haughtiness was completely out of place. One could not be in Hashem's House and offer a *korban* in a way that even slightly resembled arrogance. It would seem to completely undermine the goal of the *korban*, which was to bring a person close to Hashem. (In the same vein, we can also understand why it is forbidden to consume *chametz* on Pesach: While we are reexperiencing the *gilui Shechinah* that took place during *yetzias Mitzrayim*, arrogance is completely incongruous to that experience.)

With this perspective, we can suggest why it is so fitting that specifically the *korban minchah* for Shavuos was converted into *chametz*. Perhaps it is to alert us, on the day we commemorate *kabbalas haTorah*, to the transformational power that Torah can have. When one lives by the word of Hashem and studies the Torah, one's life is imbued with meaning and purpose—not with a superficial or artificial purpose, but a real and substantive connection to Hashem. Furthermore, Bnei Yisrael's very acceptance of the Torah demonstrated an elevated worthiness; Hashem can give the Torah only if there is someone of substance on the other end to receive it.

In a similar vein, the Gemara (*Pesachim* 68b) debates whether the Yamim Tovim are supposed to be spent *kulo laHashem*, filled with time for Hashem; *kulo lachem*, filled with time for man; or *chatzi lachem chatzi laHashem*, with time for both man and Hashem. The Gemara states that everyone agrees that Shavuos must have some element of *lachem*, time for man. Again, man must have some personal benefit on this Yom Tov, which commemorates his own agency in entering into this uplifting relationship with Hashem, and the continuous value and purpose that only the Torah provides by connecting us with Him.

· פרשת בהר ·

PARASHAS BEHAR

KI YAMUCH ACHICHA: GALUS AND GEULAH

BY RABBI BENI SELESKI

The Torah describes the sale of an individual as an *eved* (*Vayikra* 25:25–28):

כִּי יָמוּךְ אָחִיךָ וּמָכַר מֵאֲחֻזָּתוֹ וּבָא גֹאֲלוֹ הַקָּרֹב אֵלָיו וְגָאַל אֵת מִמְכַּר אָחִיו. וְאִישׁ כִּי לֹא יִהְיֶה לּוֹ גֹּאֵל וְהִשִּׂיגָה יָדוֹ וּמָצָא כְּדֵי גְאֻלָּתוֹ. וְחִשַּׁב אֶת שְׁנֵי מִמְכָּרוֹ וְהֵשִׁיב אֶת הָעֹדֵף לָאִישׁ אֲשֶׁר מָכַר לוֹ וְשָׁב לַאֲחֻזָּתוֹ. וְאִם לֹא מָצְאָה יָדוֹ דֵּי הָשִׁיב לוֹ וְהָיָה מִמְכָּרוֹ בְּיַד הַקֹּנֶה אֹתוֹ עַד שְׁנַת הַיּוֹבֵל וְיָצָא בַּיֹּבֵל וְשָׁב לַאֲחֻזָּתוֹ.

If your brother becomes poor and sells from his heritage, his close redeemer comes to him and redeems the purchase of his brother. If a man doesn't have a redeemer, but he obtains the means for his redemption; he will calculate the years of his sale and return the leftover [money] to the one who sold [the field] to him. And if he can't afford to pay him back, then the sale will remain indefinitely in the hands of the purchaser until the Jubilee year. It will go out in the Jubilee year to its inheritance.

As with all of the Torah, the above *pesukim* from *Parashas Behar* can be understood in their simple context. In this case these *pesukim* discuss the sale and eventual return of ancestral properties to their original owners. The Torah describes four stages:

1. *Ki yamuch achicha*: The sale of the property because of the seller's poverty
2. *U'va go'alo hakarov eilav*: The redemption of the land by a relative
3. *Ve'ish ki lo yihyeh lo go'el*: In the event the seller has no relative to redeem the land, the redemption of the land by the seller once he has the funds to do so
4. *Ve'im lo matzah yado*: If the land has yet to be redeemed, the return of the land to the original impoverished seller in the Jubilee year

However, the Ohr Hachaim explains that these *pesukim* are a hidden reference to Klal Yisrael's process of *galus* and *geulah*, and that these *pesukim* "*tirmoz inyan gadol ve'he'arad leyoshevei sevel*—hint at an important lesson for all of mankind." According to the Ohr Hachaim, the *pesukim* can be understood as follows:

1. *Ki yamuch achicha*: Hashem is "impoverished" on account of our sinful ways and is forced to "sell His ancestral heritage"—a reference to the destruction of the Beis Hamikdash.
2. *U'va go'alo hakarov eilav*: It is incumbent upon the tzaddikim, the *kerovim*—the close ones—of the generation to lead Klal Yisrael back to the proper path so that we will be worthy, through our *teshuvah* and good deeds, of the *geulah* and the rebuilding of the Beis Hamikdash.
3. *Ve'ish ki lo yihyeh lo go'el...vechishav es shenei*: If Klal Yisrael is not deemed worthy of the *geulah* through its *teshuvah* and good deeds, then Hashem can bring *yissurim*—afflictions of the *galus*—upon the nation as a *tikkun* to repay our debts caused by our sins and make us worthy of the *geulah*.
4. *Ve'im lo matzah yado*: If Klal Yisrael's sins are so great that even an abundance of *yissurim* can't repay the debts created by our sins, all hope is not lost. Hashem will bring the ultimate redemption and rebuild the Beis Hamikdash at a set time referred to as Jubilee.

Rabbi Yissachar Shlomo Teichtal, *zt"l*, in the first *perek* of his *sefer Eim Habanim Semeichah*, suggests that even when Klal Yisrael experiences an abundance of suffering in *galus*, this is a harbinger of the ultimate *geulah*. The prophet Zechariah refers to the Melech HaMashiach as "*ani verochev al chamor*—a humble man riding on a donkey" (*Zechariah* 9:9). The lowly donkey is a symbol for the experiences of *tzaros* and *yissurim* in our long *galus*. However, they are a sign that the wheels of our redemption are in motion and that our debts are being repaid in order to hasten the coming of the *geulah*.

· פרשת בחקותי ·

PARASHAS BECHUKOSAI

YEMOS HAMASHIACH: UNDERSTANDING THE NEW WORLD ORDER

BY STEVE KIRSCHENBAUM

The Rambam in his *sefer Yad Hachazakah* discusses all halachos—not only halachos that are relevant today, but even what we call *hilchesa leMeshicha*, halachos that are relevant only in Mashiach's times. By contrast, the Rif and the Rosh discuss only halachos that are applicable nowadays.

In *She'eilos U'teshuvos Maharik* (165) it says the reason we don't apply the halachos that are relevant to the time of Mashiach today is that the rules of *psak* will change in the time of Mashiach. The Torah doesn't change, but the rules of making halachic decisions today are relevant only for *dinim* that are applicable for our days. The *dinim* that are applicable for the future function based on different rules.

The Chida writes in the *sefer Ya'ir Ozen* (5:13) that this point is the source of a dispute between the Rambam against the Rif and the Rosh. The Rambam disagrees with the Maharik's rule and says that the halachah of our times won't change in the time of Mashiach, and the Rif and Rosh, like the Maharik, hold that the halachah will or might change. Therefore, they cannot formulate rulings for the times of Mashiach as the Rambam does.

What is this change that the Rif and the Rosh refer to based on? Will there be a change in the world when Mashiach comes? The Rif and the Rosh say that this change will be due to a change in the world order, where we'll have more *menuchas hanefesh* allowing us to understand the Torah with more clarity.

Another example illustrating the change to occur in messianic times can be seen at the beginning of *Parashas Bechukosai*. There, Klal Yisrael is promised that if they do what they are supposed to do, they will dwell securely in Eretz Yisrael, they will have no fears, and the [wild] animals will rest in the land (*Vayikra* 26:6).

What does it mean that the wild animals will rest in the land? The Ramban (ibid.) cites a dispute in *Toras Kohanim* (2:1) as to how to interpret this change. Rabbi Yehudah says it means there won't be any wild animals in the days of Mashiach. Rabbi Shimon bar Yochai says these animals will exist, but they will not harm anyone. Rabbi Shimon then asks: What is a bigger praise of Hashem, that there are no wild animals, or that the wild animals will exist, but they won't disturb people? Rabbi Shimon maintains that in the time of sitting in the land in security, the promises are about a change in the natural world order. In other words, in the times of Mashiach, there will be a change, and the world will function differently.

The Satmar Rebbe, *zt"l*, asks in his *sefer Divrei Yoel*: What exactly is that promise? He answers that it is the promise of *shalom*. We find throughout the Torah that Hashem promises that in the days of Mashiach there will be peace. We understand peace to mean the absence of war. The Satmar Rebbe says no, it's something else. It's a positive sense of *menuchas hanefesh*, peace in the sense that a person sits peacefully in his land. At that time, people will learn Torah with a different mindset. Hashem will give strength to His people and give them peace: "*Hashem oz le'amo yitein*" (*Tehillim* 29:11). Hashem will give strength of character and strength of mind, a whole different life. When we refer to *mei'ein Olam Haba*, we are talking about that type of *shalom*—one that has *menuchas hanefesh*.

Returning to the idea of the Maharik as to what actually changes during the time of Mashiach, what does he mean when he states that when Mashiach comes, the rules of *psak* will be different? His intention is that the whole mindset of *limud haTorah* will be different. The entire focus, all the pleasure, the full sense of Hashem, will be with another mentality. The Torah doesn't change, but man will be different.

The Gemara in *Eiruvin* (13b) attests about Rabbi Meir that he was greater than anyone else in his generation. If that's the case, why don't we rule according to him? The reason is that *shelo yachlu chaveirav la'amod al sof da'to*, his colleagues could not understand the profundity of his opinion. The Gemara continues and describes Rabbi Meir as being *mei'ein Olam Haba*. In this world, he had that *shalom* of *menuchas hanefesh*, allowing more clarity. That clarity will enable the rules of *psak* to change.

This world and the reality we live in detracts from our ability to have greatness in Torah. The struggle in this world is to find the peaceful moments to bolster our *mei'ein Olam Haba*.

· פרשת במדבר ·

PARASHAS BAMIDBAR

THE CENSUS AND MAN'S ROLE IN "ACTIVATING" THE SHECHINAH

BY DR. JOSHUA BROWN

Just like a person counts his money over and over again because it is precious to him, so too does Hashem frequently count Bnei Yisrael (Rashi, *Bamidbar* 1:1). Each of Hashem's censuses of the Jewish people is also connected to a monumental event, and the census in *Parashas Bamidbar,* which occurs one month after the building of the Mishkan, is no different. Rashi's description of the time line of events relating to this census, however, is perplexing:

כְּשֶׁבָּא לְהַשְׁרוֹת שְׁכִינָתוֹ עֲלֵיהֶם מְנָאָם, בְּאֶחָד בְּנִיסָן הוּקַם הַמִּשְׁכָּן וּבְאֶחָד בְּאִיָּר מְנָאָם.

When He came to place His Shechinah upon them, He counted them; on the first of Nissan the Mishkan was erected and on the first of Iyar He counted them.

Utilizing the future tense, *kesheba,* Rashi implies that Hashem's Shechinah came to dwell *after* the census occurred, which was an entire month after the Mishkan was constructed. This understanding appears to contradict several *pesukim* that explicitly link Hashem's Shechinah to the Mishkan, such as (*Shemos* 25:8):

וְעָשׂוּ לִי מִקְדָּשׁ וְשָׁכַנְתִּי בְּתוֹכָם.

Make for Me a sanctuary, and I will dwell within them.

Furthermore, on the eighth day of the Mishkan's construction, the Torah states (*Vayikra* 9:23–24):

וַיָּבֹא מֹשֶׁה וְאַהֲרֹן אֶל אֹהֶל מוֹעֵד וַיֵּצְאוּ וַיְבָרֲכוּ אֶת הָעָם וַיֵּרָא כְבוֹד ה'
אֶל כָּל הָעָם. וַתֵּצֵא אֵשׁ מִלִּפְנֵי ה' וַתֹּאכַל עַל הַמִּזְבֵּחַ אֶת הָעֹלָה וְאֶת
הַחֲלָבִים וַיַּרְא כָּל הָעָם וַיָּרֹנּוּ וַיִּפְּלוּ עַל פְּנֵיהֶם.

And Moshe and Aharon came to the *Ohel Mo'ed*. And they left and they blessed the nation. And the glory of Hashem was seen on the people. And a fire went out from before Hashem and it consumed on the altar the *korban olah* and the fats. And the nation saw, and they fell on their faces.

The Sifsei Chachamim and the Kli Yakar (*Bamidbar* 1:1) both point out that the key word to focus on in order to understand Rashi's commentary on that verse is *lehashros*, which is loosely defined as "to dwell." Hashem's Shechinah came to dwell on the very first day that the Mishkan was constructed. However, like any new construction or residency, the first thirty days were tenuous, and as such, Hashem's Shechinah, so to speak, was not yet firmly rooted there. Only after thirty days, when the Mishkan attained the halachic status of a fixed structure, did Hashem's Shechinah become a permanent dwelling, and Hashem chose to count Bnei Yisrael at that time to mark this monumental occasion.

The *sefer Ner Uziel*, by Rabbi Uziel Milevsky, zt"l, on *Parashas Bamidbar* quotes the author of the *Shem MiShmuel*, Rabbi Shmuel Bornsztain, zt"l, who also resolves the apparent contradiction as referring to two fundamentally different types of Shechinah. In Nissan, when the Mishkan was built, the Shechinah emanated solely from Hashem, irrespective of man's involvement. This is similar to the sanctity of Shabbos, which is built into the fabric of the world and arrives each week regardless of man's involvement.

By contrast, the Shechinah that came in the month of Iyar was activated by man, so to speak, as demonstrated through his involvement in the census, and reveals man's capacity to effect spiritual change. This is similar to the sanctity of Rosh Chodesh, which requires witness testimony of the new moon to establish when the month begins. These two different conceptions of the Shechinah are reflected in the astrological symbol for each month: Nissan is symbolized by a lamb, reflecting man's passive role, whereas Iyar is symbolized by a bull, reflecting man's active role.

The haftarah of *Parashas Bamidbar* suggests, however, that the task of bringing the Shechinah into one's inner sphere is accomplished not simply through external participation in a census, but also through a deep investment of one's mind and heart in coming to understand Hashem. This idea is referenced in the following *pesukim* from the haftarah (*Hoshea* 2:21–22):

וְאֵרַשְׂתִּיךְ לִי לְעוֹלָם וְאֵרַשְׂתִּיךְ לִי בְּצֶדֶק וּבְמִשְׁפָּט וּבְחֶסֶד וּבְרַחֲמִים. וְאֵרַשְׂתִּיךְ לִי בֶּאֱמוּנָה וְיָדַעַתְּ אֶת ה'.

You will be bound to Me forever. You will be bound to Me through righteousness, judgment, kindness, and mercy. You will be bound to Me through belief, and you will know Hashem.

My father, Rabbi Noach Burstein, explained to me that these *pesukim* reference different modalities of connection to Hashem. *Betzedek u'vemishpat* means coming to understand Hashem through intellectual means, through contemplation and study of His laws and justice. *U'vechesed u'verachamim* means coming to understand Hashem through emotional and spiritual means, that is, through performing acts of kindness and experiencing His compassion and mercy.

Finding connection to Hashem and developing a relationship with Him is complex, and may at times seem far-reaching and unattainable. Yet perhaps the *pesukim* are teaching us that one's focus should simply be on the process. The active engagement in the pursuit of a connection through utilizing one's intellectual abilities (*betzedek u'vemishpat*) and emotions (*u'vechesed u'verachamim*) can in turn open the door to finding faith, *be'emunah*, and ultimately to *veyada'at es Hashem*, knowledge of Hashem, and feeling His sanctity in the world.

· פרשת נשא ·

PARASHAS NASO

THE MEANING OF THE MENORAH

BY MIKE WIESENBERG

Most of *Parashas Naso* consists of a listing of the gifts the Jewish tribal leaders gave at the time of the inauguration of the Mishkan. However, after this listing, the parashah concludes with this interesting statement (*Bamidbar* 7:89):

וּבְבֹא מֹשֶׁה אֶל אֹהֶל מוֹעֵד לְדַבֵּר אִתּוֹ וַיִּשְׁמַע אֶת הַקּוֹל מִדַּבֵּר אֵלָיו מֵעַל הַכַּפֹּרֶת אֲשֶׁר עַל אֲרֹן הָעֵדֻת מִבֵּין שְׁנֵי הַכְּרֻבִים וַיְדַבֵּר אֵלָיו.

And when Moshe would enter the *Ohel Mo'ed* to speak with Him, he would hear the voice speaking to him from on top of the *kapores* which was on the *Aron*, from between the *Keruvim*, and He spoke to him.

After this statement, the next parashah, *Beha'alosecha*, immediately begins with the commandment to light the Menorah in the Mishkan. What does this statement have to do with the inauguration gifts, and why is it here?

The Netziv, at the beginning of *Parashas Beha'alosecha*, explains this concluding statement of *Parashas Naso* and its connection to the following parashah. The function of the Menorah was to serve as a conduit for Divine inspiration of Torah (specifically, the Oral Torah). In other words, Moshe would come into the Mishkan, as described in our *pasuk*, look into the lights of the Menorah, and thereby understand the Torah.[21]

---

21. The Netziv points out that Rashi in *Maseches Shabbos* (23b) states that our

The Netziv quotes the Ramban too, who famously connects the inauguration of the leaders to the commandment of the Menorah, quoting the midrash that Aharon was given the mitzvah of the Menorah as a consolation for not being a participant in the inauguration gifts. The Netziv adds that in light of this, the final *pasuk* in our parashah now fits in very well, as it connects the inauguration of the Mishkan and the parashah of the Menorah. The Menorah was not a random mitzvah, but rather a very special one that in fact is connected to the continued existence of Judaism! We shall expand on this point.

The Gemara in *Yoma* (29a) says that the miracle of Chanukah is not allowed to be written down. Why not? Rabbi Moshe Shapiro, *zt"l*, quoted in *Afikei Yam*, explains that the period of Chanukah represented a major shift in the world. This period coincided with the end of the era of the prophets, at which point Torah sages rather than prophets began to lead the Jewish people. Not only was there a shift in the Jewish world; the Vilna Gaon, in his commentary on *Seder Olam*, says the decline of *avodah zarah* throughout the world was specifically linked to the disappearance of prophecy.

It was at this juncture that a climactic battle between the Jews and the Greeks, who represented a new world philosophy, took place. The Gemara in *Yoma* (69a) says that Alexander the Great saw visions of Shimon Hatzaddik before his battles. The Gemara in *Megillah* (11a) says that Shimon Hatzaddik was the one Hashem sent to save the Jewish people in the times of Chanukah. Why Shimon Hatzaddik, who lived well before the Chanukah story? Rabbi Shapiro explains that Shimon Hatzaddik was the leader of the first generation of sages who guided the Jewish people after we no longer had prophets. He led the Jewish people into this new phase wherein we were directed by the Torah sages alone, without the aid of prophecy.

Why was the miracle of the Menorah needed? After all, while we have an obligation to do mitzvos when we can, when for some reason

---

own Chanukah menorahs serve this purpose as well.

we are unable to do a particular mitzvah, we are exempt. Furthermore, there is a principle in halachah that *tumah hutra betzibbur*, the use of impure objects is allowed for public services (*Pesachim* 77a). This means that the *kohanim* could have lit the Menorah with impure oil even if they hadn't found any pure oil at all, or if it had run out after one day.

The reason the miracle of the Menorah was needed is that the miracle was a sign. It was an indication that the Jewish people were still guided by Torah and watched over by Hashem, even though prophecy was gone and a new philosophy—that of the Greeks, exemplified by Alexander, who conquered much of the world, and his teacher Aristotle—was rampaging throughout the world.

Why was specifically the Menorah chosen? As noted before, the Menorah is the vessel in the Beis Hamikdash that represents the Divine guidance and inspiration of Torah. When we light our menorahs every year, which the Rambam says is a "very precious" mitzvah (*Hilchos Chanukah* 4:12), we are demonstrating our *emunah* in the continued guidance of Hashem via the Torah and its sages.

· פרשת בהעלותך ·

PARASHAS BEHA'ALOSECHA

THE SIGNIFICANCE OF THE MITZVAH OF THE MENORAH

BY RABBI LEVY SHEINFELD

On each of the first seven days of Chanukah, the Torah reading is from the end of *Parashas Naso*, where it describes, day by day, the *korbanos* that the *nesi'im* brought for the inauguration of the Mishkan in the desert. On the last day of Chanukah, the reading encompasses not only the completion of that section, going through the eighth day until the end of the twelve days plus the summary of all the *korbanos*, but also, curiously, a reading from the first few *pesukim* of *Parashas Beha'alosecha*. Those *pesukim* contain the commandment given to Aharon Hakohen to light the Menorah every morning. The connection to the Menorah seems straightforward enough that at least on the last day of Chanukah we can add in the reference to lighting the Menorah.

To explain the juxtaposition of these two parshiyos, the first Rashi in *Parashas Beha'alosecha* (*Bamidbar* 8:2) quotes from the *Midrash Tanchuma*. Aharon felt bad that his tribe did not participate in the *chanukas hamizbei'ach* of the other tribes; therefore Hashem told him, "Yours is greater than theirs, because you will be lighting the Menorah." Ostensibly, the compensation Hashem gave Aharon is that he would light the Menorah every evening, whereas the bringing of the *korbanos* by the *nesi'im* was only a onetime occurrence for each of them.

The Ramban on *Bamidbar* 8:2 asks why was it specifically lighting the Menorah, as opposed to any of the other *avodos* in the Mishkan—which Aharon was doing during the same time period of the Mishkan's inauguration—that would comfort and console Aharon. In addition, wouldn't the fact that the *kohen gadol* was privileged every year with performing the Yom Kippur *avodah*, an *avodah* which would be *pasul* if done by any other *kohen*, and part of which included his entering the Kodesh Hakodashim, serve as enough of a consolation for him?

The Ramban's first answer is that in fact the *pasuk* is referring to the *chanukas habayis* of the Chashmona'im, which included not only the *korbanos* and the lighting of the Menorah, but also the recognition of the miracles of the war and the salvation that occurred through the *kohanim*, the children of Aharon Hakohen. The Ramban's second answer provides a message that is relevant into our own lives today. Quoting the same *Tanchuma* that Rashi does, the Ramban points out that part of the consolation for Aharon was that the *korbanos* were brought only while the Beis Hamikdash was standing, while the candles of the Menorah are forever. But how can that be, since we don't have the mitzvah of lighting the Menorah in the Beis Hamikdash since the building was destroyed (see *Sefer Hachinuch*, mitzvah 99)? He explains that the mitzvah of lighting the menorah on Chanukah is an extension of the mitzvah of lighting the Menorah of the Beis Hamikdash. Obviously, it doesn't have the same *dinim*, but the concepts are the same. Just as the Menorah in the Beis Hamikdash was not lit to provide light (as anyway it was lit just before night, according to most opinions, when the Beis Hamikdash was then closed and locked), so too we are not allowed to benefit from the lights of our personal menorahs.

Chanukah and its mitzvos are the epitome of recognizing the *hashgachah pratis* in everything that happens, from the miracle of the victory in war, to finding the *pach shemen*, to the oil miraculously lasting for eight days. And through the *mesirus nefesh* of the Chashmona'im, we have been *zocheh* to bring the mitzvah of *Menoras haMikdash* into our homes, adding to the spiritual light that guides our lives.

· פרשת שלח ·

PARASHAS SHELACH

LESSONS IN EMUNAH FROM KALEV
AND THE MA'APILIM

BY RABBI AARON R. KATZ

The Piaseczner Rebbe, *Hy"d*, also known as the Aish Kodesh, gives a powerful interpretation of *Parashas Shelach*. The Rebbe discusses Kalev, who called to the generation of the wilderness to begin the process of conquering Eretz Yisrael: "We shall surely ascend and conquer it for we can surely subdue it" (*Bamidbar* 13:30). The other spies had already provided their frightening testimony. Kalev and Yehoshua, being the only two spies who didn't speak badly about Eretz Yisrael, were now faced with the near-impossible task of continuing to inspire the Jewish people to enter the Holy Land.

Writing in June 1940, during the torment of the early months of the Warsaw Ghetto, the Aish Kodesh asks why Kalev did not substantively address the claims of the other ten spies, but instead just called for the people to go up and inherit the land. He states:

Such must be the faith of the Jew. Not only when he sees an opening and path to his salvation, that is, that he reasonably believes, according to the course of natural events, that God will save him, and thereby he is strengthened; but also at the time when he does not see, Heaven forbid, any reasonable opening through the course of natural events for his salvation, he must still believe that God will save him and he is thereby strengthened in his faith and trust. On the contrary, at such a time it is better that he does not engage in intellectual convolutions to find some rationale and opening through natural means, since it is clear that he will not find one—consequently, it is possible that his faith will be diminished. This diminution in his faith and trust in God might serve to prevent his salvation, Heaven forbid.[22]

According to the Aish Kodesh, Kalev pointedly avoided addressing the specific claims of the other spies—because they were true! Indeed, there were challenges that Bnei Yisrael would be facing, yet Kalev nevertheless said that they should go up and take over the land, beyond reason and beyond logic. Such faith and trust in Hashem draws our salvation close.

But the story of the spies is, perhaps surprisingly, not the only case of disaster associated with a group rising up in defiance of Hashem and Moshe Rabbeinu in the context of Eretz Yisrael. A bit later in the parashah there is the difficult story of the *ma'apilim*, the group that responded to the plague in the aftermath of the story of the spies by defiantly ascending into the land against the will of Hashem, only to be subsequently struck down by Amalek and Canaan.[23] In a sense, the story of the *ma'apilim* was the perfect foil for the words of Kalev stated earlier in the parashah, as Kalev (especially as elucidated by the Aish Kodesh) represents the ultimate paragon of obedience to Hashem at all costs.

In his masterful work *Tzidkas Hatzaddik*, the great chassidic master Rabbi Tzadok Hakohen of Lublin brings an added level of nuance. In that *sefer* (ch. 46), Rabbi Tzadok notes that clearly the time was not right for the *ma'apilim* to ascend, as the *pasuk* says (*Bamidbar* 14:41):

---

22. Translation provided by Henry Abramson, *Torah from the Years of Wrath 1939–1943: The Historical Context of the Aish Kodesh* (Scotts Valley, CA: CreateSpace, 2017), 122–124. See also the text and a photograph of the actual handwritten text of the Rebbe in Daniel Reiser's *Derashot Mishenot Haza'am* (Jerusalem: Herzog Academic College/World Union of Jewish Studies/Yad Vashem, 2017), vol. 1, 144–145, and vol. 2, 30.

23. Interestingly, the term *ma'apilim* is used to refer to the Jews who illegally immigrated despite the restrictive British policy on aliyah during World War II and the years before the founding of the State of Israel.

וַיֹּאמֶר מֹשֶׁה לָמָּה זֶּה אַתֶּם עֹבְרִים אֶת פִּי ה' וְהִוא לֹא תִצְלָח.

And Moshe said, "Why do you transgress the word of Hashem?
It will not succeed."

However, there will be a different time when this approach will succeed, and this is in our time, which is the period of *ikvesa d'Meshicha*,
the heels of Mashiach.[24] According to Rabbi Tzadok, the *ma'apilim* may
have had the proper intentions, and in fact there will come a day when
their approach will indeed bear fruit, but their timing was off, and at
that point they were clearly transgressing the will of Hashem.

Taking both the words of the Aish Kodesh and Rabbi Tzadok together, perhaps that is one of our most difficult tasks during these days
of *ikvesa d'Meshicha*: striking a balance between completely submitting
our will to Hashem's while recognizing that there is room for demonstrating some of the chutzpah of the *ma'apilim*—with the caveat that we
obtain the proper guidance as to when and how to properly channel
that streak of audacity.

---

24. Rabbi Tzadok, who died in 1900, was no doubt aware of the nascent Zion-
ist movement developing in Europe, and there is certainly a widespread reading
of his words as serving as tacit support of this development. See, for instance,
Rabbi Yoel Bin Nun's article "Shelach: The Sin of the Scouts and the Events that
Followed," Torat Har Etzion, June 20, 2019, https://etzion.org.il/en/tanakh/torah/
sefer-bamidbar/parashat-shelach/shelach-sin-scouts-and-events-followed: "The
Zionist *ha'apala* has indeed succeeded with God's help, and the prophecy of R.
Tzadok Ha-Kohen has been proven true!"

· פרשת קרח ·

PARASHAS KORACH

AREN'T WE ALL HOLY?

BY DR. EZER WEISS

What was the basis for the rebellion of Korach and his followers? Notwithstanding the numerous midrashim and commentaries that deal with this question, textually we are offered only one brief *pasuk* in which Korach and his followers lay out their points of contention with Moshe and Aharon (*Bamidbar* 16:3):

וַיִּקָּהֲלוּ עַל מֹשֶׁה וְעַל אַהֲרֹן וַיֹּאמְרוּ אֲלֵהֶם רַב לָכֶם כִּי כָל הָעֵדָה כֻּלָּם
קְדֹשִׁים וּבְתוֹכָם ה' וּמַדּוּעַ תִּתְנַשְּׂאוּ עַל קְהַל ה'.

They assembled against Moshe and Aharon, and said to them, "You take too much upon yourselves, for the entire congregation are all holy, and Hashem is in their midst. So why do you raise yourselves above Hashem's assembly?"

There are four statements being made here:
1. It (i.e., your leadership position) is too much for you.
2. The entire assembly, i.e., all of us, are holy.
3. Hashem is among us (i.e., all of Bnei Yisrael).
4. Why do you exalt yourselves over the congregation?

While their referencing of statements 1 and 4 is understandable, statements 2 and 3 seem out of place. After all, do we not already know that we are all *kedoshim*, and that Hashem is among us? What is Korach, the archetypal rebel, trying to accomplish in referencing *kedushas Yisrael*?

There are several approaches to be taken in understanding this verse. Rashi makes a fascinating comment on the phrase *kulam kedoshim*. Rather than stating that it refers exclusively to an inherent level of *kedushah*, he interprets it to mean that "they all heard words at Sinai from the mouth of Hashem." In explaining Rashi, the Sifsei Chachamim states that Korach was directly contesting Moshe and Aharon's prophetic authority by arguing that because all of Klal Yisrael were also present for the revelation at Sinai, their levels of prophecy rivaled Moshe's. In other words, he was calling into question our foundational belief in the uniqueness of the Mosaic prophecy.

According to the Chizkuni (*Bamidbar* 16:3), when stating that "*kol ha'eidah kulam kedoshim*," Korach was not actually referring to the entirety of Klal Yisrael. He explains that Korach was specifically referring to the *bechorim*, the firstborns, who had previously been referred to as *kadosh* (*Shemos* 13:2). In doing so, Korach was appealing to his base by stating that the service should not have been taken away from firstborns and given to the *kohanim*. As Moshe had been the one to delegate the priestly service to Aharon and his children, Korach was effectively calling into question Moshe's true representation of Hashem's will.

The author of the *Ha'amek Davar* advocates a similar approach. He maintains that it was the 250 followers of Korach, who themselves were actually righteous, who argued that the holy service should be open not only to the *kohanim*, but to all who were worthy of it in order to facilitate their own attainment of high levels of closeness to Hashem.

The most popular approach, however, is clearly that in which Korach was actually arguing with Moshe and Aharon from a starting point that all Jews are holy. The Ibn Ezra explains that he felt this holiness took root at the time of *Matan Torah*, and that it persisted from then forward. According to Rabbeinu Bachya, the fact that all Jews are holy was the basis for Korach's argument in support of anarchy. Quoting the famous midrash, he states that Korach claimed that just as tzitzis made entirely out of *techeiles* should not need *techeiles* strings, so too a holy and noble people should not need individuals lording over them.[25]

So if we truly are a *"mamleches kohanim vegoy kadosh"* (ibid. 19:6), a royal and holy people, why was this argument wrong? Why is it that we should need appointed leaders to instruct and guide us?

In his classic work *Nesivos Shalom*, Rabbi Shalom Noach Berezovsky, the Slonimer Rebbe, *zt"l*, posits that Korach erred in two basic ways. First, he explains that Korach denied (or misunderstood) the essential, primary importance of having a unique tzaddik figure to serve as both an intermediary to allow the common Jew to serve Hashem, as well as to function as a *mashpia*, one who is able to bring down blessing and goodness from Heaven onto the common man. In contrast to this, he explains, Korach argued that because all of Bnei Yisrael were holy, and Hashem was within them, no such tzaddik was needed. This, states the Slonimer Rebbe, was an error.

Second, the Rebbe explains that Korach was of the opinion that there was no true, distinct, unified entity that could be identified as Klal Yisrael. Instead, he felt that what appeared to be a nation of Israel was merely a composite of many distinct and separate holy individuals. Given the lack of a true unified nation, he argued that a singular leader was unnecessary. In direct contrast to this, the Nesivos Shalom explains that a unique entity of Klal Yisrael does exist, and the primary *kedushah* of a Jew flows straight from the level of his attachment to this community. For the Slonimer Rebbe, the *kedushah* of the whole of the nation is greater than the sum of its parts.

Amazingly, Rabbi Yosef Dov Soloveitchik proposes an approach in direct opposition to that of the Nesivos Shalom. He maintains that Korach's error in saying that *"kol ha'eidah kulam kedoshim"* was that he meant that all Jews have an equivalent, inherent holiness which has been passed down to them *on a communal level*, from their forefathers.

---

25. Interestingly the Kli Yakar believes that Korach used this argument of spiritual equivalence to undermine the need for formal mitzvos in general (in other words, if everyone is *kadosh*, why should they require constant reminders of Hashem?) as well as the need for Hashem's very existence.

For this reason, he argued that Moshe and Aharon had no right to rule over anyone else, as their levels of holiness were no greater than anyone else's. Regarding this argument, Rabbi Soloveitchik responds that Korach erred in not realizing that there are actually two different aspects to *kedushas Yisrael*. While it is true that we do have a communal holiness which is inherited merely by dint of one being born a Jew, more importantly, each individual also has his own unique *kedushah* as well. This individual *kedushah* is commensurate with a person's religious involvement, dedication, and spiritual level obtained. For Rabbi Soloveitchik, the individual's personal *kedushah* is paramount and essential.[26]

If one takes Rabbi Soloveitchik's idea of a personal, developed *kedushah* one step further, he will arrive at the position of Rabbi Samson Raphael Hirsch. Rabbi Hirsch argues that Korach's entire premise of Bnei Yisrael containing an inherent, innate *kedushah* was flawed. He maintains that when the *pesukim* refer to us as an *am kadosh* or a *goy kadosh*, they do so as an imperative and an aspiration. The status of a Jew's being holy is not something that is automatically granted; rather, it is something that each and every individual must spend their lives striving toward, each at his own pace. As such, one clearly cannot state that because we are all holy, a leader such as Moshe is unnecessary.

Whether Korach was flawed in assuming that the Jewish people weren't in need of a rebbe, whether he underestimated the value of the communal or personal *kedushah* of every Jew, or whether he was altogether mistaken in thinking that *kedushah* was something that was automatically granted, Rabbi Hirsch makes one final point that trumps all of the others and undercuts any possible arguments that Korach may have been able to rationalize. He reminds us that Moshe was the leader of Klal Yisrael not due to the fact that he had a greater level of *kedushah* or even *nevuah* than everyone else, as true as that may have been.

---

26. These differing opinions of the Nesivos Shalom and Rabbi Soloveitchik regarding whether the communal or the personal *kedushah* is primary may be consistent with their respective chassidic versus non-chassidic worldviews.

Rather, he was the leader for the sole reason that Hashem Himself had chosen him to be so.

The underlying message is that despite what our rational thought might dictate, the only logic we need, and the only way things may, at times, make sense, is that they are all the *ratzon Hashem*. As the Mishnah states (*Avos* 2:4):

עֲשֵׂה רְצוֹנוֹ כִּרְצוֹנֶךָ, כְּדֵי שֶׁיַּעֲשֶׂה רְצוֹנְךָ כִּרְצוֹנוֹ. בַּטֵּל רְצוֹנְךָ מִפְּנֵי רְצוֹנוֹ,
כְּדֵי שֶׁיְּבַטֵּל רְצוֹן אֲחֵרִים מִפְּנֵי רְצוֹנֶךָ.

Do His will as if it is your will, in order that He will do your will as if it is His will. Remove your will for His will, in order that He will remove the will of others for your will.

Our goal should not be to question and negate Hashem's wishes; rather, it is upon us to accept them, internalize them, and make them our own. May we all be *zocheh* to strive toward and achieve high levels of *kedushah* both individually and communally, and to live in consonance with the *ratzon Hashem*.

· פרשת חוקת ·

PARASHAS CHUKAS

A LIVING CONTRADICTION: THE PARAH ADUMAH

BY RABBI AKIVA FLEISCHMANN

Parashas Chukas deals with the esoteric concept of chukim. Chukim, while generally considered to be difficult to parse, are in fact meant to be so by design. Indeed, it is Rashi himself who mentions that a chok is simply "an enactment before Me; you have no right to criticize it" (Rashi, Bamidbar 19:1).

Still, many have tried to offer at least some of their own reasoning for various chukim, or to discern their true meaning, based on their personal knowledge and intellect. However, the parah adumah resides at the top of the heap of unanswered questions. The Midrash Tanchuma (Chukas 8) tells us:

רַבִּי יוֹסֵי בַּר חֲנִינָא אָמַר: אָמַר לֵיה הַקָּדוֹשׁ בָּרוּךְ הוּא לְמֹשֶׁה: אֲנִי מְגַלֶּה לָךְ טַעַם פָּרָה, אֲבָל לַאֲחֵרִים חֻקָּה.

Rabbi Yosi bar Chanina said, "Hakadosh Baruch Hu said to Moshe: 'To you I am revealing the reason for the heifer, but to others it is an unquestioned statute (chukah).'"

The reasoning behind the chok evaded even Shlomo Hamelech, as it says in Koheles (7:23):

כָּל זֹה נִסִּיתִי בַחָכְמָה אָמַרְתִּי אֶחְכָּמָה וְהִיא רְחוֹקָה מִמֶּנִּי.

All this I tested with wisdom. I thought I could fathom it, but it eludes me.

The *Sefer Hachinuch* (mitzvah 397) quotes the *Pesikta D'Rav Kahana*, saying that what eluded Shlomo was the reasoning behind the *parah ad-umah*. But he continues and says that the reason it is listed as a *chok* is not due to its general purpose, for we find other occasions where people are ritually cleansed by means of offerings. Rather, the unknowable part is twofold: the fact that those performing the cleansing ritual were themselves rendered unclean, as well as the fact that the ritual was conducted outside of the camp (unlike other offerings), inviting others to mistake it for *avodah zarah*.

While he cannot offer a definitive reason for these aspects of the ritual, the author of the *Sefer Hachinuch* (ibid.) does put it quite beautifully as he attempts to make sense of it himself:

וְאָמְנָם כַּמָּה תְּרוּפוֹת בְּעִשְׂבֵי הַשָּׂדֶה וּבָאִילָנוֹת מִן הָאָרֶץ אֲשֶׁר בַּלְּבָנוֹן
עַד הָאֵזוֹב אֲשֶׁר בַּקִּיר מְלֵאִים סְגֻלוֹת בְּהַפָּכִים, יְקָרְרוּ הַחַמִּים וִיחַמְּמוּ
הַקָּרִים, וְאִלּוּ יָדַעְנוּ מַהוּת הַנֶּפֶשׁ וְשָׁרְשָׁהּ וּמַחֲלָתָהּ וּבְרִיאוּתָהּ, נָבִין
(בַּחְלִי) [בְּאוּלַי] כִּי סְגֻלַת הַפָּרָה גַּם כֵּן לְהַחֲלִיא הַנֶּפֶשׁ וּלְטַמְּאָהּ בְּעֵסֶק
הַשְּׂרֵפָה, וְאַחֲרֵי הֱיוֹתָהּ אֵפֶר מְרַפֵּא מַחֲלַת הַטֻּמְאָה, וְזֶה אֵינוֹ בָּרוּר
לְהַשִּׂיג בְּעִנְיָנֵנוּ כְּלוּם, אֶלָּא שֶׁחִבַּת הַקֹּדֶשׁ וְהַחֵשֶׁק לְהַשִּׂיג יְדִיעָה בַּנִּסְתָּר
יָנִיד הַקָּנֶה לִכְתּב.

And yet many medicinal herbs of the field and [medicinal] trees—from the cedars that are in Lebanon to the hyssop on the wall—are full of mysteries [that operate] in opposite [ways]. They heat the cold and cool the hot. And if we understood the nature of the spirit, its root, its illness, and its health, we would also understand [perhaps], since the mystery of the heifer is also to sicken the soul and render impure those who are involved in the burning, while its ashes heal from the sickness of impurity. This is not a clarification to provide any comprehension whatever on the matter. It is only the love of holiness and the eagerness to achieve a knowledge of the hidden that moves this quill to write.

Life is full of contrasts and seeming contradictions. How can we exist in two states of being that seem to be at odds with each other? Even the nature of the *chukim* themselves provides us with a puzzle: In the Torah given to us by Hashem, which is designed to enrich our lives, explain the rules, and provide meaning to us in our daily existence, how can there be passages whose true meanings are designed to elude us?

And yet, here we are. We are living, breathing organisms attempting to navigate the ins and outs of existence and remain true to ourselves as much as possible, even when we contradict our own natures from time to time. We witness events in our lives that boggle our minds and test the boundaries of what we think is possible. How can we exist in such a way? How can our cognitive dissonance not get the better of us?

Perhaps we can use the same vehicle through which we shrug our shoulders when we encounter *chukim* and accept them prima facie: faith. We trust, as Rashi enjoins us to, that everything that comes from Hashem has a purpose, whether that purpose is known to us or not. And even if its inherent nature appears to be self-contradictory, we know that perhaps it is not a contradiction, but a state of being that Hashem has willed into existence for a reason. *Emunah* and *bitachon* in Hashem's mysterious ways are what have sustained us for generations, and they will continue doing so, as long as we are open to allowing a little contradiction in our lives.

· פרשת בלק ·

PARASHAS BALAK

BILAM'S ADMIRATION FOR
THE TENTS OF BNEI YISRAEL

BY RABBI ARI SPIEGLER

After defeating the armies of Sichon and Og in battle, Bnei Yisrael continued their march to Eretz Yisrael. Balak, the king of Moav, saw the destruction Bnei Yisrael left and decided to enlist the help of Bilam, a prophet from Midian, to curse them. Fortunately, Hashem caused Bilam's attempts to curse Bnei Yisrael to fail, and the curses were expressed instead as blessings.

One of the more famous attempted-curses-turned-blessings was: "*Mah tovu ohalecha Yaakov, mishkenosecha* Yisrael—How goodly are your tents, O Jacob, your dwelling places, O Israel" (*Bamidbar* 24:5). The Gemara (*Bava Basra* 60a) says that this blessing refers to the wonderful homes of Bnei Yisrael, whose doors did not directly face each other. Their dwellings were the epitome of *tznius*, which Bilam saw and marveled at.

Rabbi Daniel Glatstein, *shlita*, the *mara d'asra* of Kehilas Tiferes Mordechai of Cedarhurst, notes that this is incredibly surprising and fascinating. Bilam seems to have been one of the most morally depraved human beings of all time. The Gemara (*Sanhedrin* 105b) tells us that he frequently engaged in bestiality with his donkey. Subsequently, the Gemara (ibid. 106a) suggests that after Bilam failed to curse Bnei Yisrael, he advised Balak to have the *bnos Moav* seduce the men of Bnei Yisrael to cause the latter to self-destruct.

Rabbi Glatstein says that we would have thought that a person who was so immoral and depraved wouldn't be able to appreciate the beauty and elegance of the *tznius* of Bnei Yisrael. Someone who indulged in every base urge and desire would likely mock, disapprove of, or express disdain toward *tznius*. Nevertheless, Bilam, who epitomized the antithesis of modesty, was struck by the privacy, decency, and refinement of the Jewish people. He noticed and even praised this lifestyle that was the opposite of his own. Rabbi Samson Raphael Hirsch (on *Bamidbar* 24:2) notes regarding Bilam that "he was no longer an unwilling instrument for the words that Hashem had put into his mouth."

Rabbi Glatstein urges us to take heed of this phenomenon. While we may live in times or societies that are fundamentally lacking in modesty, ensuring we conduct ourselves with *tznius* will help inspire change. We may have mistakenly thought to relax some of our own standards so as not to look foolish among the greater society. However, we see from the story of Bilam that even the most depraved person is in fact impressed and perhaps jealous of our modesty. When we carry ourselves with *tznius* it leaves an indelible mark on the world.

The same is likely true of many of the mitzvos and Torah ideals. When we practice honesty and integrity in our business dealings and social interactions, it is admired in arenas that tolerate dishonesty. When we focus on and care for the other, even the most selfish approve. When we live with *emunah* and invoke Hashem in our speech in an often faithless world, it does not go unnoticed among those who lack faith. Unfortunately, it is now considered naive, archaic, and unsophisticated to live a life of faith in Hashem. But the truth is that behaving properly influences even those who choose to live improperly.

We must never feel ashamed or frightened of personifying the ways of Hashem and His Torah, nor should we underestimate our ability to inspire change. The entire world, even those who live in direct opposition to Hashem and His Torah, are looking to us and appreciating who we are and what we do.

· פרשת פינחס ·

PARASHAS PINCHAS

PINCHAS: PURSUER OF PEACE

BY RABBI MEIR SEGAL

At the end of *Parashas Balak*, Zimri, the *nasi* of the tribe of Shimon, took Kozbi, the princess of Midian, into the *Ohel Mo'ed*, the most holy place in the desert, and publicly had relations with her. When confronted by Moshe Rabbeinu, rather than showing remorse and admitting his guilt, Zimri taunted him: "Who permitted your wife, a native Midianite, to you?" Reacting to this dramatic scene with righteous indignation, Pinchas killed both Zimri and Kozbi. Surprisingly, rather than denouncing Pinchas for taking the law into his own hands, Hashem praised him for being a *kana'i*, a zealot, and, incredulously, rewarded him by making him a *kohen* and bestowing on him "*brisi shalom*—My covenant of peace" (*Bamidbar* 25:12)! What justified Pinchas's reaction, and how was Hashem's granting him His covenant of *shalom* a fitting reward for such a violent act?

The Gemara in *Sanhedrin* (82a) teaches that a Jewish man who has relations with a non-Jewish woman is *chayav kareis*. The Mishnah in *Sanhedrin* (81b) makes an exception to this: If that same offense is performed publicly then a zealot can kill him: "*habo'el Aramis kana'im pogim bo.*" This directive is not found in a specific *pasuk* but rather is a *halachah leMoshe miSinai*, and it is not a general obligation but is limited to a *kana'i*. The reaction of Pinchas, therefore, was appropriate and in accordance with the halachah that Moshe received on Har Sinai and taught Bnei Yisrael.

Why didn't Moshe himself execute the law according to the instruction he heard directly from Hashem? The Torah relates that the reaction of Moshe and everyone present when Zimri was violating the *kedushah* of the *Ohel Mo'ed* was: "*Heimah bochim*—They were crying" (*Bamidbar* 25:6). Crying is a normal human response to an extremely unexpected situation. For a moment, unable to come to terms with what we have just witnessed or experienced, we lose our mental balance, our clarity of thinking, and we cry. By contrast, Pinchas was able to control his emotions, maintain this stability, and think clearly despite what was transpiring. Knowing that he was allowed to kill Zimri was the first step, which required *emunah* that whatever Moshe taught was dictated to him by Hashem. Having the inner strength to carry out this directive and actually kill Zimri required *bitachon* that Hashem would protect him from any negative consequences that might occur as a result of his actions.

The pursuit of peace seems to be a most honorable and popular endeavor: peace in the Middle East, peace between different opposing government factions, peace between children and parents, and so on. Who doesn't want peace? But what is the definition of this goal and how does one achieve it?

Perhaps we can receive guidance from a *tefillah* we say at least three times every day: "*Oseh shalom bimromav hu ya'aseh shalom aleinu*— He [Who] creates peace in the higher [spheres], [may] He make peace upon us."

Hashem created many powerful forces to sustain human existence, each one potentially destructive independently and beneficial only because it is perfectly balanced by Him with other equally powerful forces. We acknowledge this perfect balance as *shalom*, peace. Similarly, He created each of us with strong forces within that are vital but beneficial only if we keep them balanced properly. Perhaps the Torah's definition of a *kana'i* is a person who, because of his *emunah*, has the ability to retain *shalom*, perfect balance, under the most stressful conditions and has the *bitachon* to act decisively and to carry out the *ratzon Hashem*. Pinchas, who actualized this ability of *kana'us*, was appropriately rewarded with *brisi shalom*.

· פרשת מטות ·

PARASHAS MATTOS

NOT WITHOUT TEFILLAH

BY YOSSI SASSON

P arashas Mattos describes the army that Moshe put together when he was preparing Klal Yisrael for the battle with Midian (*Bamidbar* 31:4):

אֶלֶף לַמַּטֶּה אֶלֶף לַמַּטֶּה לְכֹל מַטּוֹת יִשְׂרָאֵל תִּשְׁלְחוּ לַצָּבָא.

One thousand for every tribe, for each tribe shall you send to battle.

The Midrash in *Bamidbar Rabbah* (22:3) comments that there are two opinions regarding how to understand this *pasuk*. One says that in reality two thousand soldiers per tribe were sent, but the second opinion says that in reality three thousand soldiers per tribe were sent: "twelve thousand for war, twelve thousand guarding their weapons, and twelve thousand for *tefillah.*" Included in this army sent to war were twelve thousand "soldiers" who were charged with davening.

Similarly, the Netziv in his commentary to *Bamidbar* 31:5 notes that when Moshe Rabbeinu sent the army out with Pinchas, he sent along "*chatzotzeros hateruah beyado*—the trumpets for sounding in his hand," and that the purpose of the *chatzotzeros* was to make a sound of a *teruah* and *tefillah.*

The Netziv states that even though Hashem promised a victory in the war, davening was a crucial component. He references his commentary to *Sefer Shemos* (14:15). As Bnei Yisrael were standing by the Yam Suf and being chased by the Egyptians with no apparent way out, the Torah says that Hashem told Moshe, "*Mah titzak eilai daber el Bnei Yisrael veyisa'u*—Why are you crying out to Me? Speak to Bnei Yisrael and travel onward." There the Netziv explains that clearly Moshe Rabbeinu was davening, and even though he knew full well that Hashem promised to save Bnei Yisrael and a *yeshuah* was sure to come, Moshe still saw it fit to daven. The Netziv goes on to say:

דְּזֶה כְּלָל גָּדוֹל בַּמִּלְחָמָה שֶׁמִּתְנַהֶגֶת בִּפְעֻלַּת הַטֶּבַע אַף עַל גַּב שֶׁבָּרוּר שֶׁיִּהְיוּ הֵמָּה מְנַצְּחִים, מִכָּל מָקוֹם צָרִיךְ תְּפִלָּה.

This is an important rule for wars that are executed within the order of nature: Even though it is clear they will win, still, prayer is needed.

The Netziv then brings a few examples, including the war with Amalek and the war with Midian in our parashah. He explains that whenever a situation is masked within nature, there is an added need for davening. By contrast, if a *nes* is required, even if the *yeshuah* is definitely going to happen, then there is no "*makom letefillah*" and he explains that is why Hashem tells Moshe at the Yam Suf, "*Mah titzak eilai.*" In other words, while Moshe thought it was a time for *tefillah*, Hashem informed him that since what was going to occur was *al pi nes*, through a miracle, there was no place for *tefillah*.

This is seemingly a very hard concept to understand, since human nature would dictate otherwise. If I need a special *nes* to assist me, apparently that would warrant *tefillah*, and if there is something I could do *al pi teva* to help myself, then while *tefillah* would be necessary, it might not be at the forefront.

Rabbi Yechezkel Levenstein, *zt"l*, in his *sefer Ohr Yechezkel* on *emunah*, brings forth another question regarding the war with Midian: Why was it necessary for the twelve thousand men who were charged with davening to go out with the soldiers? Would it not have been enough for them to stay in the camp and daven for them there?

In a different essay (*Michtavim*, no. 293), Rabbi Chatzkel explains that it is human nature to follow what one's eyes see, and therefore if the men would have stayed back and prayed in the camp while the soldiers were out fighting, people would have thought that what won the war was the fighting—the *kochi ve'otzem yadi* (*Devarim* 8:17)—and that *tefillah* was needed only to assist. As such, it was necessary to send out the twelve thousand men to pray on the battlegrounds, to show everyone that the war did not destroy the Midianites, but rather the *tefillah* did. The nation needed to see that the *tefillah* and not the actual fighting was the most integral part of winning the war. This was the only way to send that message.

I think this might be the *yesod* behind the Netziv's idea that when things happen *al pi teva*, *tefillah* is much more necessary than if a *nes* is needed. Human nature dictates that if we are making an effort *al pi teva*, it is that effort that enables us to accomplish what we set out to do, with the *tefillah* being an ancillary requirement. By contrast, with a *nes*, there is generally no room for us to make such assumptions. *Nissim* are clear directives that Hashem is in control. It is when we act *al pi teva* that *tefillah* becomes a critical prerequisite.

· פרשת מסעי ·

PARASHAS MASEI

A MOST PECULIAR TRAVELOGUE

BY RABBI AARON KRAFT

We observe a strange phenomenon at the onset of *Parashas Masei*: a detailed travelogue of the Jews' sojourn in the desert over the previous forty years. We may have found useful a brief summary, perhaps a reminder of where the journey began and where it ended. But the painstakingly detailed account recorded here seems a bit excessive. Why does the Torah devote such a significant portion of the text to listing every encampment along the way?

Rashi (*Bamidbar* 33:1) and the Rambam (*Moreh Nevuchim* 3:50), building on our Sages' interpretation that each destination came with its own set of memories, both emphasize how this list helps the Jewish people appreciate Hashem. Recollections of the miracles performed on behalf of Bnei Yisrael can inspire feelings of *shevach vehoda'ah* for the kindness Hashem showed us in the desert.

The Rambam adds that these memories document the Divine nature of the desert existence that gave birth to the Jewish nation. Embedding these memories in their minds and associating these experiences with geographic locations will enable them to pass on these traditions to their descendants, fortifying their commitment to Hashem. In this sense, the list not only engenders gratitude toward Hashem, but also fortifies the relationship with the Divine. If heretics were ever to question Hashem or His devotion to the Jewish people, accessing these memories would make us less vulnerable to their attacks.

An additional approach exists as well: The purpose is not to inspire better appreciation for Hashem, but to cultivate a stronger sense of identity within ourselves. Rashi (*Bamidbar* 33:1) quotes the midrash that records a *mashal* in which a king travels with his son to a faraway land for medical care. The journey features myriad experiences and rest stops. On the way back, as they pass back through the layovers, the king reminds his son of the experiences in each place: "Here we slept, here we were cold, here you felt ill, etc." The prince has received the necessary treatment, they've reached their destination and are on the way back home. But the king points out to his son each leg of the journey nonetheless, to teach him that the significance of a journey transcends reaching a destination. The steps along the way, the process, is just as, if not more, significant than the end point. Each juncture features shared experiences separate and distinct from the overall purpose of the journey. Those moments and memories contribute immeasurably to the identities of those involved. Similarly, Bnei Yisrael is a composite of the shared experiences they had in their nascent and formative years traveling in the desert.

The Torah relates to these vignettes from the perspective of the entire nation. But as Rabbi Samson Raphael Hirsch (ibid.) points out, "One can only surmise how many other traces of wanderings and sojourns of our forefathers may have been preserved in these places in the wilderness for the immediate and more distant future." Both as a people and as individuals, our life consists of wanderings and sojourns. The stopovers along the way, where we experience successes and failures, pride and setback, elation and disappointment, all contribute to the fabric of who we are. In this way, not only is the destination of significance, but perhaps the journey even more so.

With this understanding, we may better appreciate the inversion of a phrase that commentators notice in the context of this travelogue. The *pasuk* states (ibid. 33:2):

וַיִּכְתֹּב מֹשֶׁה אֶת מוֹצָאֵיהֶם לְמַסְעֵיהֶם עַל פִּי ה' וְאֵלֶּה מַסְעֵיהֶם לְמוֹצָאֵיהֶם.

Moshe recorded their decampments for their journeys at the

command of Hashem, and these are their journeys for their decampments.

The Kli Yakar notes on this *pasuk* that the Torah first uses the phrase "*motzaeihem lemaseihem*—decampments for their journeys" and then reverses the order and says "*maseihem lemotzaeihem*—journeys for their decampments." Perhaps this inversion indicates that the impact and significance of our journeys (as opposed to our final destination) can be felt and internalized on two planes. First, there is the decampment for the purpose of the encampment. This reflects leaving one place with the goal of setting out into new territory. As Rabbi Hirsch indicates (ibid. 33:1), a new setting provides an opportunity to attain a new goal in that setting. Each resting place provided by Hashem was suitable for a specific achievement that the people would strive for in that stage. Second, there is the journey for the sake of decampment. It takes a special ability and level of maturity and confidence to move on from one stage and enter a new one. It entails inculcating the experiences of that stage into our beings and finding the fortitude to move on and continue the journey. In this way, the act and experience of decampment provides a unique quality that contributes to our overall development.

But of course, there is one additional phrase that reveals the true key to finding success, both during the individual stages and on the journey at large: *al pi Hashem*—recognizing that the entire endeavor should be informed by and seeking the guiding hand of the Ribbono shel Olam. Even when at times the Shechinah seems absent from our journey, we believe, and sometimes in retrospect also understand, that He was with us all along. With infinite wisdom, He dictates our itineraries, knowing the significance of each destination for us and for our relationship with Him.

· פרשת דברים ·

PARASHAS DEVARIM

THE TRUE VALUE OF CHILDREN

BY RABBI BEN POMPER

Toward the beginning of *Parashas Devarim*, Moshe Rabbeinu proclaimed in his speech to Bnei Yisrael (*Devarim* 1:11):

ה' אֱלֹקֵי אֲבוֹתֵכֶם יֹסֵף עֲלֵיכֶם כָּכֶם אֶלֶף פְּעָמִים וִיבָרֵךְ אֶתְכֶם כַּאֲשֶׁר דִּבֶּר לָכֶם.

Hashem, the God of your fathers, should multiply you a thousand times as you are and bless you, as He spoke to you.

Rashi comments on this *pasuk* that Bnei Yisrael objected to the wording of Moshe's blessing. They said that Moshe was actually limiting us with his blessing, as Hashem had already promised Avraham that we would be like the dust of the earth, essentially infinite in number (*Bereishis* 13:16). They questioned why Moshe was confining our numbers to one thousand times our population then, when Hashem had promised us even more. Moshe answered that this blessing was his personal one, but indeed Hashem would bless them "as He spoke to you," in other words, that we would reach numbers that are innumerable, as was promised to Avraham.

This whole exchange seems peculiar. First, what difference does it really make if we are blessed to a number one thousand times the population of the generation of the wilderness (600,000 x 1,000 = 600,000,000, not even counting the women and children at the time) or if we are as numerous as the dust of the earth? Moshe's blessing would seem to be sufficient. Second, what exactly was Moshe's response to Bnei Yisrael's objection?

Rabbi Yissocher Frand, *shlita*, quotes the Chasam Sofer, who explains that Moshe was actually testing Bnei Yisrael regarding why they wanted children. Was their motivation simply to satisfy the emotional need that children fill for their parents? Or perhaps it was to supply the physical help that children can provide around the house or when caring for elderly parents? If these and similar motivations were driving the Jewish people's desire for children, then surely a thousand times their current population would suffice.

However, Bnei Yisrael responded to Moshe that this blessing was not enough; they didn't want to accept his limited blessing when Hashem had earlier promised them an infinite number of children. They understood that each child, each *neshamah*, brought into this world has a transcendent value that is immeasurable. The blessing of children is not to make life more convenient, or even more emotionally pleasurable for their parents. Rather, each child's *neshamah* has a unique spiritual purpose for which it comes into this world. From that perspective, any number that Moshe blessed Bnei Yisrael with would be too limiting. Only Hashem's "too numerous to count" captured the true value of each child that enters this world as part of the Jewish nation.

Rabbi Frand then explains that these contrasting attitudes toward children were manifest many years earlier in *Parashas Vayishlach*, when Yaakov met Eisav after returning from Lavan's house. Eisav saw Yaakov's family and asked, "Who are these children?" to which Yaakov replied, "These are the children that Hashem has graced your servant with" (*Bereishis* 33:5).

Pirkei D'Rabbi Eliezer explains this exchange: Eisav was questioning Yaakov. He was asking, "I thought we made a deal—I'll take this world and you'll take Olam Haba. Why do you have all these kids who are needed in this world?" Yaakov responded, "You are incorrect. Children are a spiritual gift from Hashem. Parents are given an opportunity to raise them in order for their *neshamos* to merit entering Olam Haba." Eisav's worldview was that children were practical assets for the parents in this world. Yaakov, by contrast, saw each child for his or her true, infinite worth—a pure *neshamah* that parents were entrusted with to guide on its spiritual mission in this world in order to ultimately merit entering Olam Haba.

• פרשת ואתחנן •

PARASHAS VA'ESCHANAN

NO TEFILLAH GOES UNANSWERED

BY DAVID SAMUELS

Moshe requested to be able to enter Eretz Yisrael and Hashem denied his request. This refusal requires explanation. Moshe was the greatest prophet who ever lived. Shouldn't that warrant his request being accepted? Furthermore, the Sages explain that he offered 515 *tefillos*. How could Hashem say no to all those *tefillos*? Were they all in vain? A further question is as follows: Moshe Rabbeinu posed an argument. He dedicated his entire life to Bnei Yisrael. He did everything for the *tzibbur*. He even implored Hashem to erase his name from the Torah if Hashem would destroy Klal Yisrael! How was it fair that Bnei Yisrael would merit to enter Eretz Yisrael but Moshe wouldn't? Shouldn't the plight, and also good fortune, of the representative be interwoven with those of the *tzibbur* he represents?

Rabbi Asher Weiss has a brilliant insight that shows how these *tefillos* were in fact answered: It is axiomatic that Hashem answers *tefillos*, but He does so only in a manner that He alone knows is best for the petitioner. Sometimes *tefillos* are answered directly, and the recipient receives what was requested. But other times the recipient receives something even better or that may serve a greater purpose, although he is unaware that the gift is a product of the *tefillos*.

In order to understand what the acceptance of *tefillos* means, some background information is needed. In the *Midrash Osiyos D'Rabbi Akiva* (*Batei Midrashos*, vol. 2, p. 356) it states that the current world will last for 6,093 years.[27] The *Seder Olam Rabbah* says that 2,488 years after the

---

27. Although the Gemara in *Rosh Hashanah* (9a) says that the current world will

world was created, Moshe Rabbeinu ascended Har Sinai to daven to be allowed to enter Eretz Yisrael. This would result in 3,605 years elapsing from the year Moshe made his 515 supplications to Hashem until the world's end (6,093 - 2,488 = 3,605). These 3,605 years correspond *exactly* to 515 *shemittah* cycles (3,605 ÷ 7 = 515). What is the connection between these *tefillos* and the 515 *shemittah* cycles? Rabbi Weiss explains brilliantly that these *tefillos* were used instead for a different purpose. Rather than answering favorably the specific request of Moshe, the representative of Bnei Yisrael, the *tefillos* were redirected for a more noble cause, for Bnei Yisrael themselves. Hashem uses these *tefillos* to take Bnei Yisrael back to Eretz Yisrael with the following compelling argument. He says: "Moshe, your nation will need your *tefillos* throughout the generations. I am going to take your 515 *tefillos* and apply each one to a *shemittah* cycle. Your 515 *tefillos* will carry your nation until the end of time."

Although Moshe's *tefillos* were not answered for his own benefit, they were certainly not rejected. They were reserved instead for a more noble cause, for the benefit of Bnei Yisrael, the nation that he selflessly led. It is only because of Moshe Rabbeinu's 515 *tefillos* that we have been saved as a nation time and time again, and we continue to survive our current *galus* and will persevere and thrive.

This teaches us an incredible principle: that no *tefillah* is in vain. Hashem hears our *tefillos* and answers them. We may not perceive it this way, but our perception is far from the truth.

---

last for 6,000 years, often the Gemara rounds off numbers. The more precise figure is actually 6,093 years.

· פרשת עקב ·

PARASHAS EIKEV

OUR EXISTENCE IS PREDICATED ON TORAH

BY ABE SOVA AND DR. DANI SOVA

T he Torah states, *"Lemaan hodiacha ki lo al halechem levado yichy-eh*—In order to teach you that not on bread alone can man live" (*Devarim* 8:3). Interestingly, Rabbi Samson Raphael Hirsch notes that etymologically the word *milchamah* (מלחמה), war, is derived from the root word *lechem* (לחם), bread. In truth, man's quest for bread and food is no simple task. Bread does not simply grow from the ground to be eaten and enjoyed. Man must work against whatever nature has in store while also competing with others to preserve and protect his supply.

At the same time, however, bread can reflect man's working *with* nature, in cooperation with his fellow man. Collaboratively, men utilize their intellectual and physical strengths to produce the means of their existence. They can easily adopt the motto *kochi ve'otzem yadi* (ibid. 8:17), that their strength and might are what produce their success, and mistakenly take pride in the efforts it took to provide for their own sustenance. The Torah therefore teaches that man's capacity to provide for his existence is wholly dependent on Hashem's providence. Without this understanding, man can and likely will do whatever he can to support himself and his family. By contrast, when man sees Hashem as the ultimate provider, he will recommit himself to a life devoted to Torah and mitzvos.

It is no surprise, then, that Hashem wanted the birth of our nation to be in the wilderness, wandering for forty years, solely dependent on Him for our survival. This preparatory training in the desert was meant to inculcate within us the *emunah* that our sustenance in life is solely due to Hashem's personal care and loving attention.

Rabbi Lord Jonathan Sacks points out that despite the years of hardship our nation faced throughout the forty years in the desert and throughout Jewish history, the ultimate test of our nation will be the challenge of affluence and success. It is when all our needs are met that our spiritual test begins. Assuming credit for our success blinds us to the benevolent hand behind it all.

Moshe knew there would be years of hardship, but he was more concerned about the years of plenty. In his farewell speech, he gave the Jewish people the blueprint to overcome the challenge of blessing. If an overwhelming reliance on ourselves is what steers us away from Hashem, it is an overwhelming reliance on Hashem that can maintain our spiritual commitment and unwavering devotion, despite our successes. As Rabbi Sacks beautifully said, "A society is as strong as its faith, and only faith can save a society from decline and fall. That was one of Moses's greatest insights, and it has never ceased to be true."[28]

---

28. Rabbi Jonathan Sacks, "Eikev (5771)—Why Civilisations Fail," The Office of Rabbi Sacks, August 20, 2011, https://rabbisacks.org/covenant-conversation-5771-ekev-why-civilisations-fail/.

· פרשת ראה ·

PARASHAS RE'EH

TO GIVE OF OURSELVES IS DIVINE

BY ARI BAJTNER

This devar Torah is taken in part from the late Rabbi Lord Jonathan Sacks's essay on Parashas Re'eh, "Judaism's Social Vision," published on his website on July 29, 2013.

One of the foremost tenants of Judaism is that of tzedakah. It could be said that tzedakah is the fourth leg upon which the world stands, in addition to the three listed by Shimon Hatzaddik (*Avos* 1:2). It seems appropriate that tzedakah is a fundamental article of faith in *Re'eh*, as it is the parashah that leads us into the month of Elul, which culminates in Rosh Hashanah with *U'nesaneh Tokef*'s "*U'teshuvah u'tefillah u'tzedakah ma'avirin es ro'a hagezeirah*—Repentance, prayer, and charity can avert an evil decree." But why is this so? The following *pesukim* in this parashah gives us some clues:

כִּי יִהְיֶה בְךָ אֶבְיוֹן מֵאַחַד אַחֶיךָ בְּאַחַד שְׁעָרֶיךָ בְּאַרְצְךָ אֲשֶׁר ה' אֱלֹקֶיךָ נֹתֵן לָךְ לֹא תְאַמֵּץ אֶת לְבָבְךָ וְלֹא תִקְפֹּץ אֶת יָדְךָ מֵאָחִיךָ הָאֶבְיוֹן. כִּי פָתֹחַ תִּפְתַּח אֶת יָדְךָ לוֹ וְהַעֲבֵט תַּעֲבִיטֶנּוּ דֵּי מַחְסֹרוֹ אֲשֶׁר יֶחְסַר לוֹ. (דברים טו, ז-ח)

If there is a needy person among you, one of your kinsmen in any of your settlements in the land that Hashem your God is giving you, do not harden your heart and shut your hand against your needy kinsman. Rather, you must open your hand and lend him sufficient for whatever he is lacking. (*Devarim* 15:7–8)

הִשָּׁמֶר לְךָ פֶּן יִהְיֶה דָבָר עִם לְבָבְךָ בְלִיַּעַל לֵאמֹר קָרְבָה שְׁנַת הַשֶּׁבַע שְׁנַת הַשְּׁמִטָּה וְרָעָה עֵינְךָ בְּאָחִיךָ הָאֶבְיוֹן וְלֹא תִתֵּן לוֹ וְקָרָא עָלֶיךָ אֶל ה' וְהָיָה בְךָ חֵטְא. (שם טו, ט)

Beware lest you harbor the base thought, "The seventh year, the year of remission, is approaching," so that you are mean to your needy kinsman and give him nothing. He will cry out to Hashem against you, and you will incur guilt. (ibid. 15:9)

נָתוֹן תִּתֵּן לוֹ וְלֹא יֵרַע לְבָבְךָ בְּתִתְּךָ לוֹ כִּי בִּגְלַל הַדָּבָר הַזֶּה יְבָרֶכְךָ ה' אֱלֹהֶיךָ בְּכָל מַעֲשֶׂךָ וּבְכֹל מִשְׁלַח יָדֶךָ. כִּי לֹא יֶחְדַּל אֶבְיוֹן מִקֶּרֶב הָאָרֶץ עַל כֵּן אָנֹכִי מְצַוְּךָ לֵאמֹר פָּתֹחַ תִּפְתַּח אֶת יָדְךָ לְאָחִיךָ לַעֲנִיֶּךָ וּלְאֶבְיֹנְךָ בְּאַרְצֶךָ. (שם טו, י-יא)

Give to him readily and have no regrets when you do so, for in return Hashem your God will bless you in all your efforts and in all your undertakings. For there will never cease to be needy ones in your land, which is why I command you: Open your hand to the poor and needy kinsman in your land. (ibid. 15:10–11)

The word "tzedakah" is usually translated as "charity." However, it can also mean "distributive justice; equity." The Sages interpreted the phrase *veha'avet ta'aviteinu* (ibid. 15:8) to refer to an obligation to provide the poor person with the basic requirements of existence: food, clothing, shelter, etc. At the same time, *asher yechesar lo* (ibid.) is understood to refer to a person who was previously wealthy but has now become impoverished. He too must be helped to recover his dignity.

These two dimensions of tzedakah are evident throughout its halachos. On the one hand, these halachos are directed to the reality of poverty; no one must be deprived of basic physical necessities. On the other hand, they address with sensitivity the psychology of poverty. It demeans, embarrasses, and humiliates. So tzedakah, the Sages ruled, must be given in such a way as to minimize these feelings.

The Rambam (*Mishneh Torah, Hilchos Matenos Ani'im* 10:7–14) enumerates the eight levels of charity, setting the standard for how we are to compassionately dispense tzedakah. From highest to lowest, they are:

1. One who assists a poor person by providing him with a gift or a loan, by accepting him into a business partnership, or by helping him find employment.
2. One who gives to the needy in such a way that the giver does not know to whom he is giving and the recipient does not know from whom he is taking.
3. The giver knows to whom he is giving, but the poor person does not know from whom he is receiving.
4. The poor person knows from whom he is taking, but the giver does not know to whom he is giving.
5. One who gives the poor person a gift before he asks for it.
6. One who gives only after the poor person asks for it.
7. One who gives less than is fitting but does so in a friendly and kind manner.
8. One who gives ungraciously.

The above descriptions are filled with tremendous psychological insight. What matters is not only how much you give, but how you give. The most essential idea expressed by the Rambam is that of anonymity, which in essence equals dignity. In brief, the poor must not be embarrassed and the rich must not feel superior. We give because we belong to the human covenant and because giving is what Hashem wants us to do.

Especially noteworthy is the Rambam's highest level of tzedakah: giving somebody a job, or the means to start a business. What makes poverty so embarrassing is the dependence of being beholden to others. The greatest act of tzedakah is that which enables the individual to stand on his own two feet, enabling the receiver to no longer need tzedakah anymore—so ultimately it's one of the least financially demanding forms of giving! And from the point of view of the person receiving that "charity," it is also the most dignifying because it completely removes the shame of receiving.

Another point that needs addressing is that even a recipient of tzedakah, at any level, must also give tzedakah. This begs the question: Why not skip the middleman, and have the initial giver just give the tzedakah to the third person, the ultimate recipient of the tzedakah? The answer is that the Sages understood that giving is an essential part of human dignity. The insistence that the community provide the poor with enough so that they themselves can give is a profound insight into the human condition.

Jewry has had many distinguished economists, and they have won an incredible 38 percent of Nobel Prizes in the field. Why should this have been so? Perhaps because Jews have long known that economics is one of the fundamental determinants of a society. They understand that economic systems are not written into the structure of the universe, but are constructed by human beings and can be changed by human beings, and thus that poverty is not a fact of nature but can be alleviated, minimized, reduced.

Economics is not a religious discipline. It is a secular art and science. Yet deeply underlying the Jewish passion for economics is a religious imperative: "For there will never cease to be needy ones in your land, which is why I command you: Open your hand to the poor and needy kinsman in your land" (*Devarim* 15:11).

As the gateway to Elul, *Parashas Re'eh* holds open the doors, in a way allowing for a more direct path to Hashem. It seems clear now that, at its core, tzedakah is the Torah's physical expression of the Divine act of compassion and sensitivity.

· פרשת שופטים ·

PARASHAS SHOFTIM

TAMPERING WITH TAMIM TIHYEH
IM ḤASHEM ELOKECHA

BY RABBI YONI GESSERMAN

In *Parashas Shoftim*, the Torah discusses the prohibition of attempting to learn about the future through certain mediums or nonpure methods. The segment concludes by instructing Klal Yisrael to live with an overarching principle: "*Tamim tihyeh im Hashem Elokecha—* You should be pure with Hashem your God" (*Devarim* 18:13). Rashi explains on this *pasuk* that instead of trying to divine daily events, a person should strive to be *tamim*, pure, with Hashem.

Rabbi Chaim Friedlander, *zt"l*, in his *sefer Emunah U'bechirah*, provides added depth to the instruction of the parashah by quoting Rashba's *Peirushei Aggados* (*Chullin* 7a). The Gemara in *Chullin* seems to provide a distinction between two groups of people: those who are subject to "natural" events and those subject to the principle of *ein od milvado*—translated as "there is none other besides Hashem"—due to merits gained through their Torah and mitzvos. The Rashba explains that there are two elements in this world: the element of "nature," in which Hashem set up rules of how the world works on its own, so to speak, and the element in which Hashem takes a more openly active involvement in daily events. The Rashba further explains that *ein od milvado* individuals who live with a constant connection to Torah and mitzvos can live an elevated existence, reflected in the *pasuk* "*Tamim tihyeh im Hashem Elokecha*—Be wholehearted with Hashem, your God" (*Devarim* 18:13), in which the relationship with Hashem can lift a person above what we would call "nature." However, a mundane life that does not include Torah and mitzvos can leave a person subject to natural powers, in which Hashem's involvement is hidden and distant.

The Rashba concludes by stating that the Gemara demonstrates a guiding principle in the history of Klal Yisrael. In *Parashas Lech Lecha*, Avraham Avinu had an interaction with Hashem in which Hashem "took [Avraham] outside" (*Bereishis* 15:5). Rashi says on this *pasuk* that Hashem took Avraham out of a certain *mazal* that indicated certain natural outcomes. The Rashba explains that this interaction teaches the above principle for future generations: Inasmuch as the Jewish people are connected to Hashem through Torah and mitzvos, they are no longer subject to the natural world as we see it, and instead are directly connected to Hashem and His *hashgachah pratis*.

As life events unfold around us, we seek understanding to process our deep experiences and emotions. The perspective that events are random provides neither full appreciation for life's blessings nor solace in times of great difficulty. The charge of the *pasuk* "*Tamim tihyeh im Hashem Elokecha*" is to aim to live on an extremely high level, that of Avraham Avinu. Through a commitment to Torah and mitzvos, we are able to create a connection to Hashem that will elevate us from a "natural" relationship to the world, to one that is holy and pure with an eternal purpose.

Our concluding *tefillah* is that through our connection to Hashem, we experience the appreciation in knowing that all of our blessings are sent to us from Above. In times of great sadness, we painfully request to find solace, comfort, and strength in our knowledge that Hashem's intimate involvement in our lives will lift our spirits with a sense of purity and purpose.

· פרשת כי תצא ·

PARASHAS KI SEITZEI

LO BASHAMAYIM HI

BY RABBI ZVI HERMAN

My rebbe, Rabbi Yonason Sacks, shlita, as well as Rabbi Dovid Miller, shlita, relate the following idea in the name of Rabbi Yechezkel Abramsky, zt"l.

At the beginning of *Parashas Ki Seitzei*, the Torah tells us that if a soldier sees a beautiful woman during battle and has a strong desire for her, she is permitted to him. This is known as the law of *yefas to'ar*, the beautiful captive. Rashi on that *pasuk* quotes a comment from the *Sifrei* and the Gemara in *Kiddushin* (21b):

לֹא דִבְּרָה תוֹרָה אֶלָּא כְּנֶגֶד יֵצֶר הָרַע, שֶׁאִם אֵין הַקָּבָּ"ה מַתִּירָהּ יִשָּׂאֶנָּה בְּאִסוּר.

The Torah directs its precepts against the drive toward evil, for if Hashem would not make her permissible, he would marry her in a forbidden manner.

In other words, the Torah, with its infinite knowledge of the human psyche, permitted this woman to marry a Jewish soldier because otherwise the soldier would not be able to help himself. Since it would be humanly impossible to resist this temptation, the Torah did not forbid it. The Torah therefore conceded to the *yetzer hara* in this specific scenario. The obvious question becomes: Why is this so? The Torah makes no concessions in any other realm of halachah.

Perhaps we can understand this concept a little more deeply in light of what the Ramchal, Rabbi Moshe Chaim Luzzatto, writes in *Derech*

Hashem (1:2): that the purpose of life is to be able to choose good over evil. As such, the Torah covers every aspect of human existence and outlines what is good (mitzvos) and what is evil (*aveiros*). Therefore, in every realm, we are presented with two options, good or evil, and are enjoined to choose properly.

It follows that if there is an aspect of human existence where there is no possibility at all to choose good over evil, such as in our case of the *yefas to'ar*, the Torah would not prescribe choosing good over evil. Hashem knows man's nature is such that he cannot resist this temptation, and therefore the Torah did not forbid it.

Rabbi Yonason Sacks points out that this should be a great source of *chizuk*, inspiration, to us. Very often, we view the Torah as immense, with details we cannot possibly hope to comply with. It is understood that individuals should keep as much as they can, but fulfilling the Torah in its entirety often seems an insurmountable task. Perhaps a sense of depression sets in, a lack of confidence in our ability to be complete *shomrei Torah u'mitzvos*.

The halachah of the *yefas to'ar* tells us that we can fulfill it all. If we couldn't, Hashem wouldn't ask us to. The *yefas to'ar* is the outlier, the one halachah where Hashem says, "This is too much for Me to ask of you." This implies that every other halachah in the Torah *is within man's capabilities*. The halachos of the *yefas to'ar* demonstrate that if Hashem asks us to observe a mitzvah, we must be capable of doing so. This also touches on one of the Rambam's Thirteen Principles of Faith, that the Torah given to Moshe at Har Sinai is eternal and will never be changed (see the Rambam's *Commentary on the Mishnah*, introduction to *Perek Chelek*).

May we all have the confidence and strength to continue adhering to Hashem's Torah, even in the most difficult of times.

· פרשת כי תבוא ·

PARASHAS KI SAVO

MAKING THE MOST OF YOUR INVESTMENTS

BY RABBI AVI HOCHMAN

In *Parashas Ki Savo*, the Torah speaks about the mitzvah of *bikkurim*. The farmer comes to the *kohen* (*Devarim* 26:4),

וְלָקַח הַכֹּהֵן הַטֶּנֶא מִיָּדֶךָ וְהִנִּיחוֹ לִפְנֵי מִזְבַּח ה' אֱלֹקֶיךָ.

And the *kohen* will take the basket from his hand, and place it before the altar of Hashem your God.

The Mishnah (*Bikkurim* 3:8) teaches that poor farmers would give the *kohen* both their *bikkurim* fruits and the simple myrtle baskets in which they brought them, while the affluent farmers took back their baskets of gold and silver. Why do the poor farmers' baskets remain with the *kohen*, while the rich take their baskets back?

The *Tosefos Yom Tov* (ibid.) explains that since the fruits of the poor are small and meager, we obligate them to give the fruits *and* the baskets, to make it a complete gift to the *kohen*. The rich farmers' fruit is in and of itself a significant gift, so it's enough to give just the fruit.

The Malbim (*Devarim* 26:4) teaches that there is a significant difference between the baskets of the rich and those of the poor. The poor man, he postulates, wove the basket out of myrtle branches specifically for the purpose of giving *bikkurim*. Since it was a labor of love, reflecting his personal *mesirus nefesh* for the mitzvah, the basket itself became an integral part of the mitzvah. In recognition of his noble efforts, we honor the poor person and the *kohen* keeps the basket.

My rebbe, Rabbi Benjamin Yudin, *shlita*, explains that the Torah is teaching that when one invests in something, it becomes an integral part of him. The more time, focus, and effort you put into performing a mitzvah, the more you appreciate it and the more impact it has upon you. As Rabbi Lord Jonathan Sacks explains, in the physical world, the more you give the less you have; in the spiritual world, the more you give the more you have.

Robert Arnott, an American entrepreneur and investor, once said, "In investing, what is comfortable is rarely profitable." In order to truly gain from our investments, we must go outside of our comfort zone and sincerely invest in creating a meaningful relationship with Hashem and His mitzvos. That is the poor farmer. He is the one who is willing to go out and search for meaning.

As the *pasuk* tells us (*Tehillim* 102:1):

תְּפִלָּה לְעָנִי כִי יַעֲטֹף וְלִפְנֵי ה' יִשְׁפֹּךְ שִׂיחוֹ.

A prayer for a poor man when he enwraps himself and pours out his speech before Hashem.

The Ba'al Shem Tov comments that the *tefillah* of the poor person is to be *lifnei Hashem*, before Hashem. What the poor person is looking for is to maximize his potential and invest in what truly matters: a relationship and connection to Hashem.

Throughout our lives we are faced with moments of struggle that offer great opportunity. We must constantly place our *emunah* in knowing that the right investment is with our mitzvos. The more we make the mitzvos our own, by understanding them and performing them with love and excitement, the more profitable our investments will become. These efforts will strengthen our *emunah* and our relationship with the Almighty.

· פרשת נצבים ·

PARASHAS NITZAVIM

A MITZVAH BEYOND REACH?

BY RABBI JEREMY HARTSTEIN

One of the most cryptic *pesukim* in Moshe Rabbeinu's farewell address to Bnei Yisrael can be found in *Parashas Nitzavim* (*Devarim* 30:11):

כִּי הַמִּצְוָה הַזֹּאת אֲשֶׁר אָנֹכִי מְצַוְּךָ הַיּוֹם לֹא נִפְלֵאת הִוא מִמְּךָ וְלֹא רְחֹקָה הִוא.

Surely this instruction which I enjoin upon you this day is not baffling for you, nor is it beyond reach.

The commentaries try to decipher which mitzvah Moshe was referring to here and why it was so important that the message be given over specifically at that point in time. The Ramban and Sforno are of the opinion that the mitzvah being discussed here is the mitzvah of *teshuvah*. This is based on the previous *pesukim*, where Moshe explicitly spoke to Bnei Yisrael about returning to Hashem after committing sins. Rashi, however, says that the mitzvah actually refers to the entirety of Torah, or *limud haTorah*, and observing all of its mitzvos. He bases this on the *pesukim* that follow, where Moshe attempted to strengthen Bnei Yisrael's commitment to Torah and mitzvos as they prepared to enter Eretz Yisrael.

The author of the *Kli Yakar* combines both of these approaches, clarifying the *pasuk* from each perspective. First he explains the *pasuk* from Rashi's perspective and later on from the point of view represented by the Ramban and Sforno. In explaining Rashi's position, the Kli Yakar cites the *pesukim* that follow to prove that the Torah and mitzvos are well within our grasp. This is the meaning behind *"lo baShamayim hi"* (ibid. 30:12): The Torah is not in a different world; rather, it is attainable. Hashem is promising us that His Torah was created to be utilized in this world and nowhere else. In cases where we feel that we cannot perform the mitzvos in His Torah, we have the option to learn about a specific mitzvah, and that is considered as if we have actually performed that mitzvah.

The idea that Torah is never beyond our capabilities is also expressed by Rabbi Samson Raphael Hirsch. Rabbi Hirsch says that the Torah is the greatest constant in this world. No matter what occurs and no matter what situation we find ourselves in, the Torah will always be there for us to put our complete and unyielding faith in it. Our fate as a nation is bound up with the fact that the Torah is eternal and will never be lost to us. The reason for this, explains Rabbi Hirsch, is the simple reality that the meaning of the Torah and its mitzvos, which were handed down to us through our tradition from Har Sinai, are indeed near to us and completely understandable to the human intellect: *"Lo nifleis hi mimecha velo rechokah hi"* (ibid. 30:11). There is no concept in the Torah that requires superhuman or supernatural abilities to comprehend. What we have in this world is complete and perfect. The Torah is accessible to all Jews in all parts of the world and for all times.

This explains why Moshe Rabbeinu decided to speak about that specific topic at that particular moment. Bnei Yisrael were about to enter Eretz Yisrael after spending forty years in the wilderness surrounded by miracles from Hashem. They were now moving from a supernatural existence to a more mundane lifestyle. They themselves would be forced to infuse their lives with *kedushah*. The way to do so, said Moshe Rabbeinu, was through learning the Torah and performing its mitzvos. This was not something remote or otherworldly, but right there in front of them for the taking.

· פרשת וילך ·

PARASHAS VAYEILECH

THE DEFINING CHARACTERISTIC
OF A NATION

BY RABBI DAVID PERKEL

וַיִּכְתֹּב מֹשֶׁה, אֶת הַתּוֹרָה הַזֹּאת, וַיִּתְּנָהּ אֶל הַכֹּהֲנִים בְּנֵי לֵוִי, הַנֹּשְׂאִים אֶת
אֲרוֹן בְּרִית ה', וְאֶל כָּל זִקְנֵי יִשְׂרָאֵל. (דברים לא, ט)

And Moshe wrote this Torah and gave it to the *kohanim*, the
sons of Levi, who carried the Ark of the Covenant of Hashem
and to the elders of Israel. (*Devarim* 31:9)

שָׁמַעְתִּי שֶׁאוֹתוֹ הַיּוֹם שֶׁנָּתַן מֹשֶׁה סֵפֶר הַתּוֹרָה לִבְנֵי לֵוִי, כְּמוֹ שֶׁכָּתוּב
(לקמן לא, ט) 'וַיִּתְּנָהּ אֶל הַכֹּהֲנִים בְּנֵי לֵוִי', בָּאוּ כָל יִשְׂרָאֵל לִפְנֵי מֹשֶׁה
וְאָמְרוּ לוֹ: מֹשֶׁה רַבֵּנוּ, אַף אָנוּ עָמַדְנוּ בְּסִינַי וְקִבַּלְנוּ אֶת הַתּוֹרָה וְנִתְּנָה
לָנוּ, וּמָה אַתָּה מַשְׁלִיט אֶת בְּנֵי שִׁבְטְךָ עָלֶיהָ, וְיֹאמְרוּ לָנוּ יוֹם מָחָר לֹא
לָכֶם נִתְּנָה, לָנוּ נִתְּנָה. וְשָׂמַח מֹשֶׁה עַל הַדָּבָר, וְעַל זֹאת אָמַר לָהֶם: 'הַיּוֹם
הַזֶּה נִהְיֵיתָ לְעָם' וְגוֹ' (לעיל כז, ט), הַיּוֹם הַזֶּה הֵבַנְתִּי שֶׁאַתֶּם דְּבֵקִים
וַחֲפֵצִים בְּמָקוֹם. (רש"י דברים כט, ג)

I heard that on the very day that Moshe gave the Torah scroll
to the sons of Levi, as the *pasuk* says, "And he gave it to the *kohanim*, the sons of Levi" (*Devarim* 31:9), all Israel came before
Moshe and said to him: "Moshe Rabbeinu! We also stood at
[Har] Sinai and accepted the Torah, and it was [also] given to
us. Why, then, are you giving the members of your tribe control over it, so that someday in the future they may claim, 'It

was not given to you—it was given only to us'?" Moshe rejoiced over this matter, and it was on account of this that he said to them, "This day, you have become a people [to Hashem your God]" (ibid. 27:9). [This meant:] "It is today that I understand that you cleave to the Omnipresent and desire Him." (Rashi, *Devarim* 29:3)

Moshe Rabbeinu encountered his final controversy as a leader at the conclusion of writing a *sefer Torah* and giving it to the *kohanim*. Rashi (ibid.) notes that this day was rife with conflict in that Moshe was accosted by all of Klal Yisrael, who accused him of nepotism. They declared, "We too stood at Har Sinai. Why would you assert your tribe's supremacy over us? Could it be that one day they will claim that the Torah was given to them and not us?" Rashi notes that, unlike with many of the other controversies of Moshe Rabbeinu's career, here Moshe was happy. In fact, he was so happy that he stated, "Today you are a nation," and he understood through this interaction that the Jewish people were clinging to and desirous of Hashem.

In order to appreciate the unique circumstances that caused Moshe's joy and established Klal Yisrael's nationhood, this controversy must be contrasted to a similar one. This was not the only time when Moshe Rabbeinu was accused of nepotism. Korach's virulent propagandic onslaught also included similar accusations. Not only did Korach also accuse Moshe of nepotism in appointing Aharon to the *kehunah*, but, like Bnei Yisrael in our case, he also appealed to the fact that all of Klal Yisrael was at Har Sinai to receive the Torah. If both the substance (i.e., nepotism) and the rhetoric (i.e., equality due to being at Har Sinai) are the same, then how could these two incidents yield such opposite responses from Moshe? How could Korach's rebellion be understood as a corrosive state of division, whereas Bnei Yisrael's accusation is indicative of nationhood to such an extent that it makes Moshe Rabbeinu joyous?

One could suggest that, unlike Korach's agenda, the agenda of Bnei Yisrael in our story was essentially selfless. When Korach accused Moshe of nepotism, it was in order to attain certain self-serving results. Korach wished for the *kehunah* to go to his family and for other benefits to go to his cronies. By contrast, when Bnei Yisrael challenged Moshe, they were arguing the cause of future generations. At that moment, the Torah was wholly accessible through Moshe and the pedagogical tribe of Levi. No allegations of exclusivity were voiced or even suspected. The only basis for their claim was that when the Torah was entrusted to one group, it could lead to such assertions in the distant future. Bnei Yisrael felt responsible to fight for the eternal accessibility of Torah for all Jews in future generations—for people they had never met. They needed to ensure that the very same Torah that was given to Moshe at Har Sinai was available to every future Jew that would ever exist. The authenticity of the Torah demanded it; the Jewish people were destined for it; and it was their duty to guarantee that they, the future Jewish people, would receive it, even though it served no personal benefit to the Klal Yisrael of Moshe's generation.

This quality of selflessness not only characterizes a Jewish nation, but it is also of the substance that would make a leader like Moshe Rabbeinu rejoice. When we take concern for others with such a feeling of responsibility, that is precisely what makes us who we are as a people.

· פרשת האזינו ·

PARASHAS HA'AZINU

MOTIVATING OURSELVES, MOTIVATING OTHERS

BY GAVRIEL PRERO

The ideas expressed in this essay were inspired by the shiurim of Rabbi Henoch Leibowitz, zt"l.

One of the earliest rules of parenting one learns, either through personal experience or from an experienced person, is that children are best motivated through positive reinforcement. Better to have a child work for the promise of a prize or a party than that of losing a favorite toy. Such a strategy is employed to great success in many classrooms. There are all sorts of ways children can tally up their good deeds to add up to something greater: gem jars, star charts, a Rosh Chodesh party, raffle tickets—you name it. Our *mechanchim* have gotten incredibly creative. Dangling a carrot is a very effective motivator.

As with most things in life, this idea in fact has a basis in Torah, and is even more powerful than we realize. *"Zechor yemos olam, binu shenos dor vador*—Remember the days of old; contemplate the years of each generation" (*Devarim* 32:7).

In Rashi's second explanation on this *pasuk*, he states that first, one should remember our history. Remember the times we as a people failed to do the *ratzon Hashem*, and how we were punished for that. Remember all those individuals who rose up against Hashem, and how they fared. And if this is not enough motivation, one should contemplate the future. Think about all the potential there is to amass *sechar*, and how that reward might manifest. Think about the endless blessings Hashem can bestow. Think about what awaits those who live a Torah life in Olam Haba. Think about what the world will be like once Mashiach arrives.

When thinking in terms of motivation, it makes a lot of sense that fear of retribution should be pretty effective. "Does it hurt when you do that? Yes? Then don't do that." We are expected to learn from our failures and mistakes, and from those around us whom we have witnessed fail. We often strive not to repeat the mistakes made in history. The desire not to experience pain we've had before is strong, and generally lasting.

Compare that now to the consideration of all the good that *may* happen if we do what we are supposed to. The positive outcomes are not concrete, however; they are things we must imagine. They are not things we have experienced, nor have any idea how they may manifest or when. We can only imagine what Mashiach and Olam Haba will be like, and the Sages speak of some of the details, but in truth, we don't know who will merit what, to what extent, and in what time. How is something that we can only imagine, and have no concrete visual of, supposed to not only be as equally potent as that of known punishments, but be *more* effective?

What we learn from this is a keen insight into how Hashem wired us. Humans respond to positivity. We seek grandeur; we dream, we hope. We naturally do this. We *want* to do this—even when we know what the consequences of doing wrong are, even when they are laid out for us and we've witnessed the results throughout history. The power of the potential upside, even when unknown and vague, is a far stronger motivator. Even when we have failed to learn from our mistakes or the mistakes of our people, there is hope for us yet. The dream of what is waiting for us in Olam Haba and *yemos haMashiach* can keep us on the straight and narrow.

And not only is positivity a stronger motivator than fear; fear is exhausting. We have all seen the effects of focusing on the negative. As the author sits here, writing this in the midst of the COVID-19 pandemic, we have seen how the constant onslaught of bad news and suffering can present incredible challenges to one's mental health, even if one is fortunate enough to have health for himself and his family, and to maintain sound finances. On the other hand, the "light at the end of the tunnel"—even when it's far away, even when we don't know how long it will take to get there, or whether it will even be there, or whether it will even be better—can shorten the path it takes to reach it. Not only that, but it can even bring some of that light to where there is none at the moment.

· פרשת וזאת הברכה ·

PARASHAS VEZOS HABERACHAH

A TAFKID FOR TWO WORLDS

BY TZVI HAGLER

In *Parashas Vezos Haberachah*, we reach the end of the Torah readings and prepare to begin a new cycle. We also see the transfer of authority from one generational leader to the next when Moshe Rabbeinu passed away.

Moshe was the ultimate leader and *eved Hashem*. In fact, in describing his passing, the Torah says, "*Vayamas sham Moshe eved Hashem*— And Moshe the servant of Hashem died there" (*Devarim* 34:5). *Eved Hashem* is the ultimate expression of praise for any person.

Based on this *pasuk*, the Gemara in *Sotah* (13b) brings down an opinion that Moshe didn't actually die but continued serving Hashem. The Gemara references a *gezeirah shavah* which indicates that just as regarding *Matan Torah* it says, "*Vayehi sham im Hashem*— And Moshe was there with Hashem" (*Shemos* 34:28), likewise, it says here, "*Vayamas sham Moshe eved Hashem*." We learn from this that just as Moshe was serving Hashem on Har Sinai, so too here, he was serving Hashem on Har Nevo, the mountain where he passed away. The Maharsha deduces from this gemara that even after death, Moshe was serving Hashem.

How is it possible for a person to serve Hashem after he passes away? Rabbi Yehuda Lipchitz explains as follows, based on the Vilna Gaon's commentary on *Devarim* 32:50. The best way to serve Hashem is through the mitzvos. When Hashem commanded Moshe to go up on Har Nevo to die there, this became a mitzvah for him like any other mitzvah in the Torah. By ascending Har Nevo, not only was Moshe doing a mitzvah then, but he continues performing that mitzvah until the time of

Mashiach and *techiyas hameisim*. Since Moshe is in a constant state of fulfilling a mitzvah, he continues serving Hashem even in death. Similarly, the Maharsha explains based on the Gemara in *Sotah* above that Moshe is referred to as being an *eved Hashem* even after death, as even now, Moshe is serving Hashem.

We too must strive to be like Moshe and fulfill Hashem's mitzvos at all times, not only during our lives, but even after we die, which is possible if we truly serve Hashem at all times while we are alive. Rabbi Elchanan Wasserman, *Hy"d*, teaches a similar lesson based on the Rambam (*Hilchos Teshuvah* 5), who states that each person is capable of being a tzaddik like Moshe Rabbeinu. He explains that while there never was, nor will there ever be, another *navi* like Moshe (*Devarim* 34:10), who was the ultimate *eved Hashem*, nevertheless, we can all do our utmost to be the best individuals we can be.

In explaining the relationship between Yissachar and Zevulun, Rashi states (ibid. 33:18) that Yissachar and Zevulun made a partnership wherein Zevulun would work and financially support Yissachar, who would sit and learn Torah. Rabbi Yaakov Kamenetsky, in his *sefer Emes LeYaakov*, ponders the reward that Zevulun received through this relationship. He says that Zevulun received reward not only for the mitzvah of *talmud Torah*, but he even acquired the Torah itself that Yissachar learned, so that he also became a *talmid chacham*.

Rabbi Yaakov comments that this interpretation is perplexing. How can a person who did not learn acquire the Torah that someone else learned? He explains as follows. The Gemara in *Niddah* (30b) states that a fetus is taught all the Torah in the womb and then forgets everything at birth, and a person needs to spend his or her whole life trying to return to that prenatal level of knowledge. Similarly, regarding the Zevulun person, although he was not *zocheh* to be involved in actual *talmud Torah* all day, his efforts in business and his support of the Yissachar person are likewise considered as if he is striving to return to his status before birth, where he knew *kol haTorah kulah*. The point is to struggle to return to that status; the relationship of the businessman to the yeshivah and personal dedication and support of *talmud Torah* enable him to acquire not just the reward, but the Torah itself.

Regardless of our individual *tafkid*, we should endeavor to be all we can be. Whether we are learning full-time in yeshivah like Yissachar, or are working and able to support *limud Torah* like Zevulun, each of us can strive to actualize our potential and become an *eved Hashem*.

CPSIA information can be obtained
at www.ICGtesting.com
Printed in the USA
BVHW031812090222
628491BV00001B/55